Robot Journalism
Can Human Journalism Survive?

Robot Journalism
Can Human Journalism Survive?

Noam Lemelshtrich Latar
Interdisciplinary Center Herzliya, Israel

World Scientific

NEW JERSEY · LONDON · SINGAPORE · BEIJING · SHANGHAI · HONG KONG · TAIPEI · CHENNAI · TOKYO

Published by

World Scientific Publishing Co. Pte. Ltd.

5 Toh Tuck Link, Singapore 596224

USA office: 27 Warren Street, Suite 401-402, Hackensack, NJ 07601

UK office: 57 Shelton Street, Covent Garden, London WC2H 9HE

Library of Congress Cataloging-in-Publication Data

Names: Latar, Noam Lemelshtrich, 1945–   author.

Title: Robot journalism : can human journalism survive? /
      by Noam Lemelshtrich Latar, Interdisciplinary Center Herzliya, Israel.

Description: New Jersey : World Scientific, [2018]

Identifiers: LCCN 2018003394 | ISBN 9789813237339 (hc : alk. paper)

Subjects: LCSH: Journalism--Technological innovations. | Artificial intelligence.

Classification: LCC PN4784.T34 L38 2018 | DDC 070.4/3--dc23

LC record available at https://lccn.loc.gov/2018003394

British Library Cataloguing-in-Publication Data

A catalogue record for this book is available from the British Library.

Cover design: Michael Latar

For any available supplementary material, please visit
http://www.worldscientific.com/worldscibooks/10.1142/10913#t=suppl

Desk Editors: Herbert Moses/Sylvia Koh

Typeset by Stallion Press
Email: enquiries@stallionpress.com

Preface

Artificial Intelligence (AI) is changing all aspects of communications and journalism as automatic processes are being introduced into all facets of classical journalism: investigation, content production, and distribution. Traditional human roles in all of these fields are being replaced by automatic processes and robots.

Media companies are increasingly "employing" robot journalists to discover hidden trends and insights by analyzing huge data bases, and write narratives without human involvement. The great economic efficiency of these robots can be expected to have a great appeal to the stockholders of these media companies.

Arguably, the introduction of AI and robots into traditional functions of the journalists, such as investigative journalism and storytelling, poses a serious threat to the professional future of human journalism and its primary mission as guardians of democracy. Yet, Artificial Intelligence has serious limitations, and these are creating new opportunities for human journalists to thrive and compete with their robot competitors. In fact, if understood by journalists, these limitations can empower rather than replace them and other human content creators. As New Media technologies and applications are transforming the nature of the journalistic storytelling to fit the demands of new generations of media consumers, the new journalism story can be expected to become a mix of technologies and applications that are beyond the capabilities of current AI robot journalists.

The book has two sections: The first section focuses on a discussion of AI, the new emerging field of robot journalism, and the opportunities that AI limitations create for human journalists. The second section offers examples of the new journalism storytelling that empower human journalists through the use of new technologies, new applications, and AI tools. While this book focuses on journalism, the discussion and conclusions are relevant to all content creators, including professionals in the advertising industry, which is a major main source of support for journalism.

About the Authors

Noam Lemelshtrich Latar (NLL) is the Founding Dean of the School of Communications at IDC Herzliya (Israel's first private university), which has been the site of pioneering experiments in employing cutting-edge communications technologies to synergize journalism, robotics, virtual reality, augmented reality art and conflict resolution.

NLL served as the Chairperson of the Israeli Communications Association (ISCA) from 2009 to 2012.

He received a Ph.D. in Communications from MIT in 1974, M.Sc. from Stanford in 1971, and a B.Sc. in Engineering from California State University Northridge (summa cum laude).

He was among the founders of the Community Dialogue Project at MIT, experimenting with interactive communications involving communities through electronic means. NLL pioneered the papers on touch-screen feedback for interactive TV, on new media and cybernetic decision making, on digital identities (Social DNA), and on Artificial Intelligence robotics in journalism.

NLL initiated the teaching and research of new media at The Hebrew University of Jerusalem and at Tel Aviv University, and was involved in the Israeli high-tech industry, establishing several communications startups in cognitive enhancement that employ computer algorithms and data mining for the creation of digital consumer profiles.

NLL is the Chair of the Daniel Pearl International Journalism Institute. His current research interests are the effects of artificial intelligence on media and journalism and the potential of art to create dialogue across cultures.

Amir Ruskin spends much of his time on his motorcycle and is always waiting to go outdoors with his Jeep .... Amir specializes in Information and Analytics technologies and Strategies. Gaining long years' experience in some of the largest and more complex organizations in Israel and Europe, Amir has vast experience in data and analytics challenges, from BI to AI.

Amir has led organizational changes related to decision-making processes, performance management and everything relating to management by facts. His achievements include forming the Information and Statistics Division in the Central Bank of Israel, the Global Information Center in Teva Pharmaceuticals, as well as additional major revolutions in some of the largest organizations in Israel and Europe (Air France, Texaco, Bank Hapoalim, C.A.L. to name few) as well as emerging new economy global hi-tech companies such as Credorax.

Amir is heavily involved in the Israeli startup nation; he was co-founder of HyperRoll Inc. in the 2000s (acquired by Oracle in 2009) and, lately, co-founder of Shoodoo Analytics, a Data Science-as-a-Service platform, which was funded by Israel's Innovation Authority as part of a national incubator.

Amir graduated from the Israeli army computer science school ("Mamram"), has academic degrees in Computer Science, Economics and Human Resources. Amir is also a certified Mediator.

Dr. Doron Friedman is a Professor at the Sammy Ofer School of Communications and Head of the Advanced Reality Lab (http://avl.idc.ac.il). His Ph.D. thesis, carried out in Computer Science in Tel Aviv University, studied automated cinematography in virtual environments. He continued as a Post-Doctoral Research Fellow in the Virtual Environments and Computer Graphics Lab at University College London, working on controlling highly immersive virtual reality by thought, using brain–computer interfaces. In addition to his academic research, Friedman has also worked as an entrepreneur in the areas of intelligent systems and Internet, and his inventions are the basis of several patents and commercial products.

Since 2008, Dr. Friedman and his lab members were involved in several national and international projects in the areas of telepresence, virtual reality, and advanced human–computer interfaces. His research is highly multi-disciplinary, and has been published in top scientific journals and peer reviewed conferences, including

Artificial Intelligence, Human Computer Interaction, Journal of Neural Engineering, Journal of Neuroscience, and the *Proceedings of the National Academy of Science* (PNAS). The lab's research is often covered by national and international media outlets, including CNN, BBC, *New Scientist, National Geographic,* and *Scientific American.*

Candice Kotzen, the research assistant of Dr. Friedman, is a graduate of the Sammy Ofer School of Communications at the Interdisciplinary Center (IDC) Herzliya, specializing in Interactive Communications. Ms Kotzen is currently doing research toward a master's of Arts at the Bob Shapell School of Social Work at Tel Aviv University, specializing in Trauma and Crisis.

Dr. Gali Einav is Head of the "Upstart" Entrepreneurship Minor Track program at the Adelson School of entrepreneurship at the Interdisciplinary Center (IDC) in Herzliya. She holds a Ph.D. in Interactive Television from Columbia University and has served as an Adjunct Professor of Digital Media at IDC Herzliya since 2008 and at Yeshiva University's master's in Marketing program since 2016. Dr. Einav's research interests include the impact of digital transformation on media industries and consumer behavior. She is an Advisory Board member for Nielsen Innovate, an early stage investment arm of Nielsen. Previously, she worked in the Business Planning and Development team at Canoe Ventures, a consortium of US cable operators developing interactive ad formats for live television. Prior to that, Dr. Einav led the Digital Insights and Innovations Research group at NBC Universal, overseeing strategic, business and consumer research across digital platforms.

Nathan Lipson is the founder and CEO of Perpetix, a startup that's building the first global publisher-to-publisher syndication network. Before that, for almost 17 years, Lipson was a correspondent and an editor at *TheMarker,* Israel's leading business publication, and writes commentary for journal. He was a researcher at the Bank of Israel's research department. Nathan has a B.A. in Economics and International Relations from The Hebrew University in Jerusalem and an M.B.A, from Tel Aviv University. He co-authors papers on news-related technologies. Lipson's main areas of interest are internet, media and new technologies.

Yair Galily, Ph.D. is an applied sociologist, mass media and management researcher and founder of the *Sport, Media and Society* (SMS) Research Lab at the Sammy Ofer School of Communications, Interdisciplinary Center (IDC) Herzliya. His research interests lie in the area of sociology of sport and especially sport and mass media. He has collaborated actively with researchers from around the world in several other academic disciplines. Recently he guest-edited numerous leading international journals, among them *American Behavioral Scientist* ("Sport and Global Terrorism" Sage, 2016), *Television & New Media* ("Soccer World Cup and Television" Sage, 2015), and *Online Information Review* ("Texting, tweeting and playing: sporting mega events in an online environment" Emerald, 2016). Lieutenant Colonel (Res.) Galily serves as chief (Organizational and Instructional) sociologist of the Israel Defense Forces Combat Fitness Center.

Acknowledgments

First and foremost, I would like to thank the authors who contributed their time, knowledge, and insights in their respective chapters. I would also like to thank my local Israeli language and technical editors Ms. Renee Hochman and Ms. Sara Levi for their assistance, and my son Michael Latar, for the design of the book cover.

Special thanks to the World Scientific team for their care, enthusiasm and efficient support throughout the book publication process.

Contents

Section One:
AI and Journalism

Chapter 1

Introduction

Noam Lemelshtrich Latar

Artificial Intelligence (AI), smart algorithms, and automatic processes are penetrating all aspects of human communications and human organizations, dramatically changing media platforms as well as the relations between the media and their consumers. The potential loss of human jobs as a result of such automation has become a major global issue. According to leading forecasters, almost 50% of current human jobs are at risk [Rainie and Anderson, 2017]. In this book, I have chosen to focus on the future of human journalism in the coming era of AI and automation. The potential elimination of human journalism poses real dangers to Western democracy, even to the point of endangering democratic societies' survival. The book is also relevant to other human content producers to whom it offers a more optimistic perspective on the opportunities that AI offers.

AI is frequently defined as the science of making machines do things as if they were done by humans [McCarthy *et al.*, 1955]. Today, AI algorithms are being applied to perform all aspects of human journalistic activities: gathering data, analyzing the data to reveal new insights and trends, and composing narratives. In today's era of IoT — the Internet of Things — sensors are being embedded into all objects that surround us and continuously collecting information about us, whether we are active or passive. Our mobile phones increasingly monitor our physical movements and our cellular activity, and all of this information is stored in "data silos".

Concurrent with the growing volume of information stored in these data silos, AI engineers are creating smart algorithms that can "crawl" these data silos to discover insights and trends. In 2014, Prof. Alex Pentland, a leading global expert on big data and AI, described the current developments as the emergence of a new field he termed "social physics". Pentland claims that every human activity leaves a digital trace that, for the first time, makes it possible to study human nature like we study physics through the study of atoms. We will be able to study about human nature dynamically, across billions of people, not from what people say but from what people actually do.

The sensors that are embedded everywhere around us enable the generation of digital profiles for almost every human being on the planet. Due to the dramatic reduction in the cost of DNA analysis, which is expected to drop below USD 100 in the near future [Keshavan, 2017], these digital profiles, also termed Social DNA [Lemelshtrich Latar, 2004], may include not only the digital traces of web behaviors and records of our movements but also our genetic profiles.

The algorithms that AI engineers are developing for analyzing the data silos are termed data analytics tools. Today, the capabilities of these tools and their efficiency in analyzing even greater volumes of data that include visual information is being significantly augmented by another major development in the form of tools that automatically tag media content (texts, pictures, sound, and video) on all platforms [Lemelshtrich Latar and Nordfors, 2009].

Another major development in the penetration of AI into human journalism is algorithms that convert data to journalistic narratives automatically, an innovation pioneered by two American companies, Narrative Science and Automated Insights. Today, 12 companies around the globe [Graefe, 2016] are developing AI story-writing algorithms or "robot journalists" [Lemelshtrich Latar, 2015]. Robot Journalism started in sports, then moved to the financial fields and now is used in almost all fields of human journalism activity in increasingly sophisticated ways. Hammond of Narrative Science claims that his robots can adjust the tone of the stories to the digital profiles of the individual customer [Carter, 2013]. Associated Press (AP) is already publishing thousands of stories that are being written by robots each quarter. Although the developers of robot journalists declare that their intentions are not to replace human journalists but to assist them in writing their stories, there are concerns that these algorithms will replace human journalists as media companies search for more efficiency and greater ROI for their stockholders. When asked what he would have done differently in the digital transition, in hindsight, Arthur Sulzberger, the publisher of *The New York Times,* responded, "Hire more engineers" [cited in Doctor, 2013, para. 1].

State-of-the-art innovations in AI may soon enable fully automatic news rooms in which robots have replaced key human functions: editors, journalists, and marketing personnel. Ray Kurzweil, inventor and Chief Google Futurist, predicts that by 2029, computers will be able to do whatever we humans can do, but better [Levy, 2013]. Daniel Kahneman, 2002 Nobel laureate in economics, recently agreed with Kurzweil: "Will there be anything that is reserved for human beings? Frankly, I don't see any reason to set limits on what they [the robots] can do. We have in our heads a wonderful computer; it is made of meat, but it is a computer. It's extremely noisy, but it does parallel processing. It is extraordinarily efficient. There is no magic there. So it's very difficult to imagine that with sufficient data there will remain things that only humans can do" [Kahneman, 2017]. Is this also true in the field of human journalism? This is the central question of this book. If Kurzweil and Kahneman are right, human journalism will cease to exist.

One way to address the question of whether robot journalists can replace human journalists is to explore whether AI has limits, and whether these limits offer new horizons for human journalism.

Since the foundation of AI 70 years ago, the founding fathers of AI, John McCarty, Herbert Simon, and Marvin Minsky, and their followers have, since the 1950s and early 1960s, predicted that all the problems of AI would be resolved within 20 years. Now, 70 years later, despite important recent developments in deep learning and neural networks, everyone realizes that the human brain is far more complex than was presumed [Knight, 2016].

A contrasting school of thought rejects the AI predictions voiced by advocates such as Kurzweil and Kahneman, that the artificial brain will eventually surpass the human brain in all fields of activity. Leading linguist and AI philosopher John Searle claims that the artificial brain, which comprises electronic hardware, will never be able to fully emulate the biological activity of the human brain. According to Searle, AI algorithms can instruct computers to perform simple electronic activities, but computer algorithms cannot develop emotions [Searle, 2013]. Margaret Boden, a leading researcher on creativity and AI, studied the potential creativity of AI and predicts that, in the foreseeable future, the artificial brain will not be able to attain the highest level of creativity attained by the human brain. She posits that algorithms will attain this highest level of creativity ("transformational creativity") when they are able to transform a conceptual space that extends beyond the conceptual space defined by the algorithm's creators [Boden, 2004].

Nancy Andreasen, a leading scholar of creativity and the human mind, claims that the high intelligence that AI algorithms represent is of limited use in tasks that involve creativity: Beyond a certain IQ, genius creativity is not directly related to IQ because the highest level of creativity occurs when the brain goes through free associations and irrational thinking processes [Andreasen, 2014]. In contrast, current AI algorithms process information based on rational decision-making processes: Artificial "neurons" pass information to other "neurons" only if such information reduces uncertainty.

If we accept the lines of thought led by Seale, Boden, and Andreasen, the human brain has a major advantage in the realms of high creativity in the current state of electronic hardware and structure of artificial neural networks. This is good news for human journalists.

Another limitation of AI algorithms is that they perform their analysis within predefined conceptual spaces yet are unable to benefit from the "wisdom" of other algorithms applied to other fields, which is why current AI research is known as Narrow AI or Weak AI. There are no current AI algorithms that can perform integration across separate AI fields. AI algorithms that are able to perform such integration, or "General AI", are not expected in the foreseeable future [Dickson, 2017]. "Super AI" refers to a machine brain that will be far more powerful than the human brain, triggering what Kurzweil describes as the Age of Singularity, beyond which forecasting the future is not possible.

Another important development for human journalism's survival is the ever-changing nature of the "architecture" of the journalism story and consumer media consumption behaviors of different age groups. For example, members of the "Z Generation" (individuals born after 1996) demand fewer texts, more visual content, and more interactivity. The new mode of storytelling that developed in response to this demand involves an integration of new platforms, new immersive technologies such as Virtual Reality (VR) and Augmented Reality (AR), and applications in a way that generates a dynamic type of immersive consumer engagement. The current Narrow AI is incapable of creating the new journalism story that today's consumers expect, which is a fusion of innovative technologies and applications. If and when General AI becomes the standard, this situation may change, but it is not expected in the foreseeable future. The human journalists are adaptable to such new demanding storytelling technologies.

The book is divided into two sections: The first section is devoted to a discussion of AI robotic journalism and related issues. The second section illustrates storytelling in the era of new journalism in different journalistic fields, offering practical examples to journalists of how to create journalism stories and continue to hold their jobs in the coming AI and Automation decades. A special chapter is devoted to an analysis of AI from a systems perspective as it penetrates governing organizations. For such organizations that generate huge amounts of data in their daily routine activities and assimilate automation into all aspects of their decision making processes, introduction of AI algorithms is a matter of their survival, yet not without problems. Human journalists should be well aware of and address the dangers that AI algorithms pose to such governing organizations and society as a whole.

Chapter 2 is devoted to a discussion of AI and concepts such as deep learning, neural networks, singularity, and other recent efforts to fully emulate the human brain. Two schools of thought on whether the artificial brain can replace the human brain in the foreseeable future are discussed, together with a clarification of the concepts of

"Narrow AI", "General AI", and "Super AI" and the obstacles to Natural Language Processing or NLP projects. The chapter addresses the limitations of AI, with a special focus on creativity, intuition, and rationality, and the opportunities they open for human journalism.

Chapter 3 is devoted to recent developments in the automatic conversion of data to narratives and stories, which is referred to in the literature as robot journalism. What began in 2010 as a university experiment has developed into a big business. Twelve companies in all leading world economies are already active in the automatic conversion of data to journalistic stories without human involvement, and many millions of content units are being produced by robots for news channels and advertising. The ultimate objective of these companies is to automatically generate stories that uniquely match the digital profiles of consumers.

Chapter 4 addresses the concepts of Big Data, data mining, data analytics tools, the Cloud revolution, AaaS (analytics as a service), data monetization, and the concept of SoLoMo (Social, Local, Mobile). Employment of data analytics tools in investigative journalism is a condition for human journalism's survival in its competition with robot journalists. The data analytics tools described in this chapter illustrate the diverse array of tools that are now available.

Chapter 5 describes the coming Automatic Newsrooms, in which all functions currently performed by humans, including journalists and editors, will be replaced by robots. The chapter discusses the road map leading to full automation: automatic tagging of all media contents, algorithms that create digital profiles of consumers based on their web activity, and the architecture of the AI engines that employ machine learning algorithms for content targeting to consumers based on their digital profiles. The world has already adopted a universal standard to make the introduction of these digital profiles more efficient.

Section 2 of the book is devoted to the emerging new journalism story, a development that gives human journalists a clear advantage over robot journalists.

Chapter 6 explores the "new journalism story" and how it is affected by the new technologies and applications. Significant changes in consumer media consumption behavior have occurred across different age groups, and specifically their adoption of platforms such as Facebook, Snapchat, Instagram, Twitter, and WhatsApp. The chapter offers examples of how storytelling is being reinvented by, for example, Snapchat's 10-second stories, Vine's 6-second stories, or YouTube's "bumper ads", which require new story formats. The authors discuss how gaming, the new 360° virtual videos, and "chatbots" are changing storytelling, and the implications of such changes. In the foreseeable future, AI algorithms will be unable to comprehend and integrate such a mix of technologies and applications in order to tell compelling stories using contemporary formats, opening up an important opportunity for human journalists.

Chapter 7 is devoted to the exciting new VR and AR technologies that are creating a new field of journalism storytelling known as immersive journalism. Young generations demand — and the competition for consumers' attention requires — constant efforts to enhance consumers' media experiences, whether they consume the news or advertising. For the first time, VR and AR technologies promise a seamless holistic experience, and total immersion in a story, and these technologies are being integrated into the stories of all major media companies. This chapter describes these technologies and illustrates how VR is being used in major news stories. VR and AR technologies provide the human journalists with an important edge over their robot journalist competitors as the use of immersive technologies to tell a story remains beyond the capabilities of Narrow AI.

Chapter 8 offers examples of how AI has already begun to impact war coverage news stories. AI algorithms and new digital devices are dramatically changing journalists' roles in coverage of conflict zones. This chapter discusses the new synergy between human journalists who cover conflict zones and robot journalists. Research shows that journalists who cover war zones may compromise their professional ethics in war coverage due to a host of reasons, including fear for their lives or emotional involvement in the scenes unfolding before them. In fact, almost one third of these journalists suffer from trauma for the rest of their lives. New data collection technologies, big data and data analytics tools, and automatic narrative software can improve the depth of the war coverage stories and save journalists' lives and mental well-being. In exchange, journalists who cover conflict zones must adapt to the new storytelling paradigms.

Chapter 9 is devoted to the new sports journalism story. No other journalism field is being so dramatically affected by AI and new visual technologies as sports news. The new immersive technologies of VR and AR now allow consumers to experience themselves as part of the story in their own living rooms, and at the same time they have access to sophisticated data analysis that combines live data with historical data of each move on the sports field. This chapter tells the story of the introduction of AI into sports reporting, and focuses on the human advantage in light of the efforts in the past to enhance the viewing experience by combining multiple visual technologies on the screen.

Chapter 10 is focused on human journalists who cover political issues related to organizational and government decision-making processes in the age of AI and automation. The cybernetic model of social decision making is employed as an illustration of a framework of analysis that facilitates in-depth understanding of how organizations operate and make decisions. The chapter is devoted to an analysis of AI as it penetrates governing organizations that introduce automation into all aspects of decision-making processes, primarily to deal with the huge amount of data they accumulate during their daily routine activities. The social development theory offered in this chapter argues that automation is "the universal law of social development". Human journalists must be aware of and address the effects and specifically the dangers of introducing automation in decision-making processes.

References

Andreasen, N. C. (2014). Secrets of the creative brain. *The Atlantic*. Retrieved from http://www.theatlantic.com/features/archive/2014/06/secrets-of-the-creative-brain/372299/

Boden, M. (2004). *The Creative Mind: Myths and Mechanisms*. London: Routledge.

Carter, J. (2013). Could robots be the writers of the future? *techradar.com*. Retrieved from http://www.techradar.com/news/computing/could-robots-be-the-writers-of-the-future-1141399

Dickson, B. (2017). What is narrow, general and super AI. *Tech Talks*. Retrieved from https://bdtechtalks.com/2017/05/12/what-is-narrow-general-and-super-artificial-intelligence/

Doctor, K. (2013). The newsonomics of "Little Data," data scientists and conversion specialists. *NiemanLab*. Retrieved from http://www.niemanlab.org/2013/10/the-newsonomics-of-little-data-data-scientists-and-conversion-specialists/

Graefe, A. (2016). Guide to automated journalism. *Tow Center for Digital Journalism, Columbia Graduate School of Journalism*. Retrieved from https://www.cjr.org/tow_center_reports/guide_to_automated_journalism.php

Kahneman, D. (2017). *Remarks* [Video File]. NBER Conference Toronto: Economics of AI Conference. Toronto. Retrieved from https://digitopoly.org/2017/09/22/kahneman-on-ai-versus-humans/

Keshavan, M. (2017). Illumina says it can deliver a 100USD genome soon. *STAT*. Retrieved from https://www.statnews.com/2017/01/09/illumina-ushering-in-the-100-genome/

Knight, W. (2016). AI winter isn't coming. *Technology Review*. Retrieved from https://www.technologyreview.com/s/603062/ai-winter-isnt-coming/

Lemelshtrich Latar, N. (2004). *Personal Psycho-social Web-derived DNA & Socio-cybernetic. Decision*. Be'er Sheva, Israel: Burda Center for Innovative Communications Publication, Ben-Gurion University.

Lemelshtrich Latar, N. (2015). The robot journalist in the age of social physics. In G. Einav (Ed.), *The New World of Transitioned Media* (pp. 65–80). Basel: Springer. doi:10.1007/978-3-319-09009-2.

Lemelshtrich Latar, N. and Nordfors, D. (2009). Digital identities and journalism content. *Innovation Journalism*, 6(7), pp. 4–47.

Levy, S. (2013). How Ray Kurzweil will help Google make the ultimate AI brain. *Wired*. Retrieved from https://www.wired.com/2013/04/kurzweil-google-ai/

McCarthy, J., Minsky, M. L., Rochester, N., and Shannon, C. E. (1955). *A Proposal for the Dartmouth Summer Research Project on Artificial Intelligence*. Retrieved from https://www. cs.swarthmore.edu/~meeden/cs63/f11/AIproposal.pdf

Rainie, L. and Anderson, J. (2017). The future of jobs and job training, *Pew Research Center*. Retrieved from http://www.pewinternet.org/2017/05/03/the-future-of-jobs-and-jobs-training/

Searle, J. (2013). Consciousness and the brain [Video file]. Retrieved from https://www. youtube.com/watch?v=j_OPQgPIdKg&ab_channel=TEDxTalks

Chapter 2

Are AI's limitations creating new opportunities for human journalists?

Noam Lemelshtrich Latar

Journalism is a combination of art and science. The artistic nature of journalistic work is manifested in the search for new creative ideas, new creative angles to cover a story, new thoughts, new solutions to problems, and new ways of enriching the lives of audiences. The scientific part of journalistic work involves the use of analytical tools to support and validate information and ideas on the basis of data silos where human activity is recorded and stored. Current Artificial Intelligence (AI) algorithms provide human journalists with data analytics tools to explore and identify insights from huge data silos, and also provide journalists with algorithms to write basic narrative texts, but such algorithms lack the ability to enrich a journalism story using the mix of innovative technologies and applications that is demanded by the younger generations.

1. How Intelligent is Artificial Intelligence?

Scientist John McCarthy, considered one of the founders of Artificial Intelligence (AI), coined the term in 1955, and defined AI as the "science and engineering of making intelligent machines" [McCarthy *et al.*, 1955]. AI is frequently defined as the science of making machines do things as if they were done by humans. A key question being discussed by scientists and philosophers today centers on whether a machine "brain" can emulate the human brain and its creativity. Can AI algorithms develop cognition in a manner that allows an algorithm to "think" outside itself, or are algorithms confined to programs and lack those dimensions of human thoughts that are strongly linked to human creativity, such as intuition, feelings, and the subconscious [Andreasen, 2014]? The answer to this question is highly relevant to many areas, including the future of human journalism in the age of AI and robot journalism.

From the dawn of AI, scientists who developed AI algorithms did so with the ultimate aim of emulating the human brain. A vital element in AI is the important contribution of English statistician, philosopher, and Presbyterian minister Thomas Bayes (1702–1761), who developed the foundation for the theory that incorporates uncertainty into decision making and problem solving. Smart algorithms are programmed to assign probabilities to specific events. They are designed to "learn from experience" (heuristically) and gradually reduce uncertainty levels of events over time, consequently creating new knowledge. In contrast to "ordinary" algorithms that are sets of instructions for a computer to execute in a predetermined order, a Smart AI algorithm is not programmed to perform the same actions every time, but varies itself in unpredictable ways based on a learning process. The strength of smart algorithms is derived from their ability to process very complex situations by scanning huge data silos with many variables, at very high speeds.

Due to the very high speed of current computer technologies, Smart AI algorithms can process and analyze databases that are virtually unlimited in size, and identify statistically significant connections among data elements. AI algorithms are great tools for testing hypotheses created by scientists, or even for proposing new hypotheses based on their findings (to be examined by future research). They are a great human invention for knowledge expansion, but these "connections" must be properly validated if they are to add real value to human knowledge.

Some leading philosophers of science resist the idea that an artificial brain could ever replace human biological brains. This issue has great relevance for whether computers can be creative, and to what extent robot journalists could ever replicate the creativity of human journalists. John Searle, one of the world's great philosophers of mind, language, and AI, is one of the leaders of this group. In a 1990 paper published in *Scientific American*, Searle provides a detailed argument why computers are "not playing that game" of replacing the human mind. In contrast to several AI scientists who believe that the right programs with the right inputs and outputs can create minds, Searle [1990] claims that computers cannot "think". He rejects that the famous "Turing Test" measures human intelligence and cognition: In his opinion, it merely tests simulations.

To understand Searle's arguments, it is important to understand his definition of a computer program:

> Digital computers merely manipulate formal symbols according to rules in the program...just manipulating the symbols is not by itself enough to guarantee cognition, perception ,understanding, thinking...programs are defined in terms of symbol manipulations, and the symbols are purely formal, or syntactic...they have no essential physical properties... and are manipulated without reference to any meanings... formal symbol manipulation... is not sufficient to guarantee the presence of meaning or semantics ... the only power that symbols have...is the power to cause the next step in the program when the machine is running...the only relevant properties of 0's and 1's are abstract computational properties and they are already well known [1990, pp. 26–27].

Searle criticizes AI philosophers who believe that the mind is a separate entity from the biological brain and therefore can be fully programmed. According to Searle, human brain thinking processes involve neurobiological processes that cause consciousness and other mental phenomena, which can explain feelings, pain, thirst, smell, and love. The manipulation of symbols by computers cannot, he argues, produce neurophysiological processes in the brain and therefore cannot produce cognition, which is a biological phenomenon. In a TED talk, Searle [2013] repeated the major arguments in this 1990 paper, concluding that "We cannot build a conscious machine".

One contemporary thinker who disagrees with Searle is Ray Kurzweil, a leading global visionary theoretician and developer of AI who is now the Chief Google Futurist. Kurzweil is a credible inventor of numerous world-changing technologies including the first flatbed scanner, the first computer program able to recognize typeface, and the first text-to-speech synthesizer, to name but a few of his many inventions. Several of Kurzweil's earlier predictions have been successful. When a *Wired* interviewer asked Kurzweil whether he would attribute consciousness to a system that really understands complex natural language, he responded:

> Well, I do. I've had a consistent date of 2029 for that vision. And that doesn't just mean logical intelligence. It means emotional intelligence, being funny, getting the joke, being sexy, being loving, and understanding human emotion. That's actually the most complex thing we do. That is what separates computers and humans today. I believe that gap will close by 2029 [cited in Levy, 2013].

What Kurzweil refers to is the ability of the AI algorithms to understand human emotions by analyzing facial expressions, behavior, or texts — but will this ability make the AI algorithm itself emotional? It may allow the AI algorithm to better monitor human needs and become more efficient at decision making and problem solving. Nobel Laureate Daniel Kahneman agreed with Kurzweil's predictions at a recent NBER Conference on AI, stating, "Will there be anything that is reserved for human beings? Frankly, I don't see any reason to set limits on what they can do. We have in our heads a wonderful computer, it is made of meat but it is a computer. It's extremely noisy, but it does parallel processing. It is extraordinarily efficient. There is no magic there. So it's very difficult to imagine that with sufficient data you there will remain things that only humans can do" [Kahneman, 2017]. Kahneman's focus is on decision-making processes and therefore considers whatever disrupts pure rational decision-making processes as "noise". Kahneman predicted that the robot brain will eventually surpass the human brain in its capacity for rational decision making, and he attributes the machine brain's potential superiority to eliminate the "extreme noise" that disrupts and undermines rational thinking in the human brain. Kahneman [2017] calls for replacing human decision makers with algorithms whenever possible. "Even when the algorithms don't do very well, humans do so poorly and are so noisy that just by removing the noise you can do better than people".

However, it may be this very "noise" in the human brain that is responsible for great human inventions. As we discuss below, high creativity has been directly linked to irrational decision processes. There is much more to human culture and soul than efficient decision making and predictions.

Earlier predictions made by the founders of AI, who were great innovative scientists, indicate that they may have underestimated the complexity of human psychology or brain. For example, in 1956, John McCarthy, the father of AI, said: "To make machines use language … a significant advance can be made … if a … selected group of scientists work on this for a summer" [McCarthy *et al.*, 1955, p. 12]. In 1965, Herbert Simon, one of the founders of AI and recipient of the 1978 Nobel Prize in Economics, stated, "Machines will be capable within 20 years of doing any work a man can do" [cited in Gaskin, 2008].

It may not be surprising that the definition of AI is dynamic and changes with time. " …it is constantly redefined to describe things we don't yet know how to do well with computers. Things like speech recognition (like Siri), image recognition (face recognition in consumer cameras), and the like used to be hard AI problems. As they become practical commercial offerings, they spin off as their own disciplines" [Smith and Anderson, 2014]. Searle already commented on this phenomenon in his 1990 paper on the limitations of AI. He stated, "Workers in AI complain — correctly — that this is a case of moving goalposts. As soon as an AI simulation succeeds, it ceases to be of psychological importance….". For example, the game of chess is frequently mentioned as an example of AI at its best. The algorithm studies numerous possible moves and based on past probabilities of success of each possible move determines what should be its next move. Today, however, it is now argued that the chess algorithm is so mechanical that it should no longer be considered AI.

2. Neural Networks

AI scientists' ultimate goal of emulating the human brain led algorithm developers to create algorithms that imitate the information processing method "used" by the neurons that make up the nervous system in the human brain. These algorithms, called neural networks, operate within an Artificial Neural Network (ANN), which is "an information processing paradigm that is inspired by the way biological nervous systems, such as the brain, process information. The network is composed of a large number of highly interconnected processing elements (neurons) working in parallel to solve a specific problem" [Stergiou and Siganos, 2011, para. 1.4]. The "learning process" in an ANN involves a huge number of binary comparisons that the information processing elements stored in the memory of the system perform almost at a speed of light.

Incoming signals are received in artificial "dendrites" that transfer the new information to the artificial "cell body", which sums these signals. Only if the total sum of the information exceeds a certain threshold are the signals transferred through artificial axons to other information processing neurons. Thus, as more information is received, threshold levels change, and uncertainty is gradually reduced (see Figure 1). The previously stored information in the cell body plays a key role in this process.

An ANN is composed of hierarchically ordered layers of neurons. The process of how an artificial neuron processes information is explained in a description of the efforts of Hinton and other researchers to develop an efficient way to teach

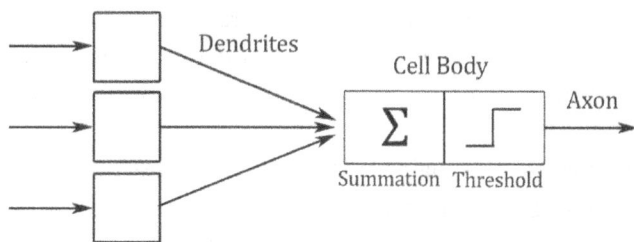

Artificial Neuron

Figure 1.   Illustration of an artificial neuron.

individual layers of neurons. "The first layer learns primitive features, like an edge of an image or a tiniest unit of speech sound. It does this by finding combinations of digitized pixels or sound waves that occur more often than they should by chance. Once that layer accurately recognizes those features, they are fed into the next layer which trains itself to recognize more complex features, like a corner or a combination of speech sounds. This process is repeated in successive layers until the system can reliably recognize phonemes or objects ... like cats" [Hof, 2013].

Neural networks thus depend on past behavior of the systems and the probability of connections between their various elements. The artificial neuron is updated every time it encounters new information but will not pass the information to other neurons if the connections between the elements are at the level of "chance". This is typical of rational thinking. In our conscious rational thinking processes, we are willing to learn only from new information that we view to be above a level of chance.

In his 1990 *Scientific American* paper, Searle claimed that the ability of neural networks to process information or computation in parallel and in multiple layers does not change his arguments that machines cannot create consciousness. The ANN paradigm enhances the efficiency of what he calls "manipulation of symbols", yet does not add meaning to the symbols.

3. Singularity

Borrowing from science fiction writer Vernor Vinge who, in 1993, predicted that within 30 years, "we will have the technological means to create superhuman intelligence. Shortly after, the human era will be ended" [Vinge, 1993, p. 11]. Kurzweil defines singularity as "the moment in the future when men and machines will supposedly converge". Singularity is a singular event "in the sense that it happens once in human history" [Eder, 2003, para. 3]. The age of singularity is also described as a "post-human era" beyond which further predictions will not be possible: "Singularity is meant as a future time when societal, scientific and economic change is so fast we cannot even imagine what will happen from our present perspective ..." [Eder, 2003]. This is the first time that forecasting theorists have put a limit on their ability to forecast beyond unimaginable new futures as mankind is expected to transform to a new "post-human" entity.

Kurzweil declared that his main objective at Google is to develop algorithms that understand natural language, which he sees as the key requirement for AI to expand knowledge and for his forecasts to materialize. "I have a one sentence (job) spec which is to help bring natural understanding to Google .... Google will know the answer to your question before you asked it" [cited in Cadwalladr, 2014, para. 24]. At Google, Kurzweil has access to an amount of data unprecedented in human history.

4. Deep Learning and Neural Networks

Every query posed to a search engine elicits millions of possible answers or links. Current search engines base searches primarily on keywords in the queries because they do not "understand" the meaning of our requests. As a result, search is an inefficient process. The aim of a relatively new field of AI research known as "Deep Learning" is to create an artificial human brain that will be as similar as possible to the human natural brain. The objective of Deep Learning is not only to have AI — such as search algorithms — understand meaning but also to "make inferences and decisions on its own" [Hof, 2013]. Basically, Deep Learning adds greater depth to the analyses performed by neural networks by adding additional "layers" of analysis. Deep Learning, which is made possible by improvements in mathematics and the increasing power of the computers, has achieved notable advances in speech and image recognition.

The invention of "Deep Learning" ended what many AI scientists termed "the AI winter", and spurred expectations that Deep Learning would finally realize the AI vision of creating an artificial brain stronger than the human brain. The fathers of deep learning are considered to be Geoffrey Hinton, David Rumelhart, and Ronald Williams, who published a paper on the topic in 1986 [Somers, 2017]. Hinton is currently the lead scientist at the Google Brain AI team, of whom it is stated, "…nearly every achievement in the last decade of AI — in translation, speech recognition, image recognition, and game playing — traces in some way back to Hinton's work …. In 30 years we're going to look back and say Geoff [Hinton] is the Einstein — of AI, deep learning, the thing that we're calling AI" [Somers, 2017, para. 2].

The basic idea behind the Deep Learning concept is "back propagation", which was invented by Hinton and his colleagues in 1986. In back propagation, when a neural network tries to identify a given object (a sentence, for example), it runs an analysis through the different layers of the system until it reaches a final binary decision as to how to tag or identify the object. If the identification was wrong the system tracks back, from the end result through the analysis, to identify and correct the errors made at each stage. This reversed process allows the system to correct and learn from its mistakes. Such a process of correcting previous errors in comparison to real facts is yet another feature of a rational thinking procedure.

Deep learning methods are being developed and used today by Microsoft, IBM, and others. IBM developed the famous Watson algorithm that has been made available to different industries and helps medical doctors in their diagnoses and assists lawyers and journalists by automatically analyzing texts to discover arguments for or against specific issues (the "Watson Debater") (http://www.kurzweilai.net/introducing-a-new-feature-of-ibms-watson-the-debater).

A major issue related to AI that is causing major concerns is decision making, and specifically the inability of the engineers who developed the Deep Leaning algorithms to explain the decisions that are made by the algorithms. "It is a problem that is already relevant, and it's going to be much more relevant in the future," says Tommi Jaakkola, a professor at MIT who works on the applications of machine learning. "Whether it's an investment decision, a medical decision, or maybe a military decision, you don't want to just rely on a 'black box' method" [cited in Knight, 2017, para. 5]. As a result of the integration of AI algorithms into all government decision-making processes, government officials will be hard pressed to explain the considerations behind their decisions, or be accountable for their decisions. "There's already an argument that being able to interrogate an AI system about how it reached a decision is a fundamental right. Starting in the summer of 2018, the EU may require that companies be able to give users explanations for decisions that automated systems reach" [Knight, 2017, para. 6].

Sommers, author, programmer, and a technological reviewer for *MIT Technology Review*, agrees with Searle and Boden (see below) about the limits of current AI research and that algorithms will nonetheless remain within the boundaries of symbol manipulation, despite the advance made in the development of Deep Learning and Neural Networks: "Neural nets … represent, at best, a limited brand of intelligence, one that is easily fooled. A deep neural net that recognizes images can be totally stymied when you change a single pixel, or add visual noise that's imperceptible to a human" [Somers, 2017, para. 26].

5. Holistic Computing: IBM's Neurosynaptic Chip

In 2014, IBM introduced a new neurosynaptic computer chip that is designed to overcome the limitations of the AI processes using traditional computers, by integrating the capabilities of the left brain (language and analytical thinking of traditional computers) and the capabilities of the right brain "with the hope to meld the two capabilities together to create a holistic computing intelligence … at unprecedented scale" [IBM Research, 2014].

IBM's long-term goal is to build a chip with "ten billion neurons, one hundred trillion synapses, occupying less than two litters of volume" — an artificial brain that will be very close in its behavior to the human brain. The IBM brain is expected to play an important role in research and industrial applications in many areas including "public safety, vision … health monitoring and transportation" [IBM Research, 2014]. To achieve this goal, IBM is developing sophisticated software agents or sensors, called cogs, which will be embedded in all human environments to create "cognitive offices", "cognitive mobile phones", "cognitive cafés", and "cognitive homes". These cogs will collect information on our dynamic cognitive decision making in these environments, in order to feed the artificial brain. IBM calls this ecosystem "the society of cogs". Furthermore, in this "society of cogs" ecosystem, cogs will both follow and interact with humans and other cogs [IBM Research, 2013].

Although the IBM "brain" will arguably be more efficient in speed and energy consumption compared to any AI algorithms ever developed, the transfer of information from one nerve cell to another will still follow the ANN paradigm, which depends on knowledge thresholds, previous information, and new information defined in terms of above-chance probabilities. The IBM "brain" can be expected to be very efficient and assist the human journalists in discovering new insights, but with limited capacity to write quality news stories.

6. The Three Levels of AI

Three levels of AI are discussed in the literature: Narrow AI, General AI, and Super AI. Narrow AI (also known as Weak AI) is an algorithm that can perform a single task, such as image recognition, weather forecast, finding insights in data silos, or playing chess [Dickson, 2017]. The algorithm "works within a limited context and cannot take tasks beyond its field" [Dickson, 2017, para. 10].

General AI (also known as human-level or Strong AI) are algorithms that "can understand and reason its environment as a human would" [Dickson, 2017, para. 13]. General AI can process information across fields, "juggle between multiple unrelated thoughts and memories when making a decision ... think abstractly ... innovate, come up with thoughts and ideas that have no precedence. Think about the invention of the telephone, ships, telescopes, concepts such as mail, social media, gaming, virtual reality. It's very hard to teach a computer to invent something that isn't there" [Dickson, 2017, para. 14]. Finally, Super AI will be algorithms that can be more creative than human brains, a state that corresponds to what futurists term the age of singularity. Despite all the progress that has been made to date, including the introduction of neural networks and deep learning methods, the most sophisticated algorithms today constitute Narrow AI.

7. Can AI be as Creative as a Human Being?

The ability of smart algorithms to create new knowledge raises a serious question: Can these rational processes lead to unexpected creative ideas or solutions? Can AI algorithms be creative? This question is of critical importance to all future jobs, including human journalism.

Today, AI algorithms are being used in many areas, including the arts, music composition, and other fields of human creativity. The products of these art algorithms are displayed in museums, and robotic music is played in concert halls. Let's take a look at two examples of the use of algorithms in the arts.

Harold Cohen is a master in integrating the human psychology and AI. Cohen has been developing an algorithm (AARON) that generates paintings in his own style or in the style of major artists, in line with the algorithm's instructions; Artwork by AARON is now found in leading museums. Cohen started to develop the AARON in 1973 and it kept improving over time [Moss, 2015]. The AARON algorithm in itself is creativity and innovation at its best, but describing the random products of his algorithms as creative art would be similar to describing the beautiful outcomes of the rotation of the Kaleidoscope as "creative" arts. It was the creation of the kaleidoscope and its internal geometry that was the truly creative innovation, not the random results of rotating the kaleidoscope. Even Cohen himself has never described his paintings in terms of creativity.

Another example is the music algorithm developed by Cope [1996]. Cope developed algorithms that can compose new music based on the styles of the great masters of music, and he described his work as "experiments in musical intelligence". Nonetheless, similar to the kaleidoscope example, the true creation is the algorithm itself and not the music compositions whose tones are selected according to the instructions of an algorithm.

In 2016, Google announced Magenta, a new ambitious project of the Google Brain Team. The Magenta project aims to "create compelling art and music" with two main objectives: to advance machine learning for music and art generation and to cultivate a community of artists, coders, and machine learning researchers [Eck, 2016]. According to Eck, "The scope of Magenta has always been about art in general, storytelling, music, narrative, imagery and trying to understand how to use AI as a creative tool" [Metz, 2017, para. 6].

Margaret Boden, a leading theoretician on AI and creativity, and the author of *The Creative Mind: Myths and Mechanisms* [Boden, 1990], argues that creativity is more than merely generating new combinations of ideas. Boden proposes a theory for creativity that provides a good framework for analyzing AI creativity. Her model comprises three levels of creativity: combinational, exploratory, and transformational [Boden, 2009]. While acknowledging that AI algorithms involve the cognitive dimension of creativity, she argues that AI is inherently limited in emulating human creativity due to "the difficulty of approaching the richness of human associative memory, and the difficulty of identifying our values and of expressing them in computational form" [Boden, 1998, p. 349].

The combinatorial technique is most commonly used for generating new insights using AI. AI algorithms of this type study associations between data elements stored in huge data bases (such as Google) and use these associations to generate new insights (these insights still need to be validated before they can be considered to have value). According to Boden [1998], the AARON automatic robot art generator, discussed earlier, is an example of exploration, the second level of creativity, which entails a search for creative ideas by exploring a predefined conceptual space. According to Boden, the exploration algorithm is not truly creative: "AARON cannot reflect on its own productions, nor adjust them so as to make them better. It cannot even transform its conceptual space, leaving aside the question of whether this results in something better" [1998, p. 353]. The fact that the AARON algorithm cannot be creative beyond the conceptual boundaries defined by Cohen leads Boden to conclude that "We cannot expect real breakthroughs from them… almost all of today's creative computers are concerned only with exploring predefined conceptual spaces… no fundamental novelties or truly shocking surprises are possible." This finding has significant implications for human journalism, which are discussed below.

Douglas Eck of the Google Magenta Project seems to agree with Boden. In a September 2017 interview with Rachel Metz on the question of why Google AI is still unable to tell a joke, Eck says, "I think it's unlikely to me that a machine learning algorithm is going to come along and generate some transformative new way of doing art. I think a person working with this technology might be able to do that. And I think we are so, so, so far from this AI having a sense of what the world is really like … most of what we do is sitting in a genre we kind of understand …" [cited in Metz, 2017]. Eck's remarks have far reaching implications for the future of human journalism in the AI age. Eck is acknowledging human superior creativity but adds that a person wishing to be highly creative at the transformational level should use AI tools. Somers concurs that the current state of the art emphasizes both the potential of AI and its limitations. "Indeed, almost as often as we're finding new ways to apply deep learning, we're finding more of its limits … Machines have trouble parsing sentences that demand common-sense understanding of how the world works … Deep learning in some ways mimics what goes on in the human brain, but only in a shallow way — which perhaps explains why its intelligence can sometimes seem so shallow" [Somers, 2017].

Leading neuroscientist Nancy C. Andreasen [2014, para. 8] describes the results of her many years of research studying the secrets of the creativity of the human brain. She describes her research topic as "the science of genius, trying to discern what combination of elements tends to produce particularly creative brains … what, in short, is the essence of creativity?". Andreasen conducted brain scans and long in-depth interviews with a very select group of outstanding globally known scientists, mathematicians, artists, and writers who ostensibly are considered creative geniuses and confirmed that IQ is not a good predictor of creativity. Her finding supported a previous finding by Lewis M. Terman, a Stanford psychologist and author of

Genetic Studies of Genius, who conducted his research in the early twentieth century, and developed one of the early IQ tests that came to be used extensively in the USA. In his very select group of gifted children, Terman [Andreasen, 2014, para. 17] found that high IQ did not predict high levels of creative achievement later in life: "Only a few made significant creative contributions to society; none appear to have demonstrated extremely high creativity levels of the sort recognized by major awards, such as the Nobel Prize …". Andreasen describes other studies that reinforced Terman's conclusions and the "threshold theory", which claims that above a certain level, intelligence has little effect on creativity.

Andreasen [2014, para. 40], like many researchers before her, came to the conclusion that "unconscious processes are an important component of creativity … observing which parts of the brain are most active during free association would give us clues about the neural basis of creativity". In contrast to Kahneman, who considers such factors as "noise", Andreasen's research links high levels of creativity to irrational thinking, free association, and unconscious human brain processes. Many of her subjects told Andreasen that their "eureka" moments came when they were showering, driving, or exercising, or during an afternoon nap, which is a further indication of the importance of the interaction between the subconscious and the conscious thought processes in the creative process that occurs in the brain. Another finding was that creative people have broad interests and are active in many fields; many were adventuresome and not risk averse. Andreasen also found that family environment affects the creativity of the family members: High achieving families positively affect creativity of their family members. Her study also revealed the importance of multidisciplinary education (rather than focusing on either the arts or the sciences) and encouraging children to "think different", to borrow from a famous saying attributed to Steve Jobs.

Interestingly, Andreasen [2014] also found a high correlation between creativity and some form of mental illness. This was true with artists and scientists. The most-common diagnoses Andreasen describes include bipolar disorder, depression, anxiety or panic disorder, alcoholism, and schizophrenia.

8. Can AI Programs Intuit?

The fact that intuition plays an important role in human creativity leads to another important and relevant question: Can AI developers program intuition? If not, can AI algorithms be creative without intuition?

The Merriam Webster dictionary defines intuition as "a natural ability or power that makes it possible to know something without any proof or evidence: a feeling that guides a person to act a certain way without fully understanding why" (https://www.merriam-webster.com/dictionary/intuition). Frantz [2003, p. 266] describes how Herbert Simon, one of the founding fathers of AI and recipient of the Nobel Prize for Economics in 1978, attempted, over his long career, to remove the mystery surrounding intuition and creativity, and offers an explanation of what intuition is not: "Intuition is not a conscious analytical — logical, sequential, step-by-step, and reasoned — process of thinking … [it is] a gut feeling, educated hunch, sixth sense".

Simon was one of the early developers of the chess algorithm and was able to mimic the mind processes of the masters of chess. He attributed chess players' success to their ability to store in their subconscious game patterns and their corresponding values. The ability of the chess masters to quickly decide the next chess move from their subconscious led him to define intuition as "subconscious pattern recognition based on experiences stored in memory and retrieved when needed" [Frantz, 2003, p. 270].

According to Simon, humans and machines conduct similar thinking processes in decision making: First they study data and search for patterns; the patterns are stored in the memory; and these stored patterns are then used in the decision-making processes. Simon concluded that intuition and analysis are not two independent processes but rather two complementary components that are essential in effective decision-making systems. Simon concluded that "Intuition is actually analytical thinking frozen into habit and into the capacity for rapid response through recognition of familiar kinds of situations" [Simon, 1997, p. 139].

Simon assumed that with sufficient data and clever algorithms, intuitive thinking is programmable by AI scientists as he was successful in programming the intuitive processes of chess masters. Whether we will be able to fully program intuitive processes and thus make an artificial brain that is as or more creative than the human brain still remains more in the realm of science fiction. A scientific answer will require scientific research of enormous scope.

9. Understanding Human Natural Language

Another serious limitation of AI is related to the limited ability of AI algorithms to understand natural language, especially contextual information, metaphors, humor, and poetry. There is an ongoing philosophical debate among scholars as to whether machines will ever be able to fully understand the richness and depth of natural language within continually evolving cultural and social contexts.

All the major digital superpowers have invested billions of dollars in the field of natural language processing (NLP) in an effort to understand human natural language in depth. Natural language processing is the ability of a computer program to understand human speech, not merely translate words. The challenge is in preserving the meaning of sentences, which requires "the automation of any or all linguistic forms, activities, or methods of communication, such as conversation, correspondence, reading, written composition, publishing, translation, lip reading, and so on" [Novoseltseva, 2017, para. 3].

Terry Winograd, a leading researcher in human language processing, knowledge representation, and AI, claimed that AI's understanding of natural language cannot extend beyond a bureaucratic level similar to "… a person without empathy, that acts according to some strict mechanic rules" [Trausan-Matu, 2005, p. 5]. According to Winograd [1991, p. 199] "… artificial intelligence as now conceived is limited to a very particular kind of intelligence: one that can usefully be likened to bureaucracy in its rigidity, obtuseness, and inability to adapt to changing circumstances". A current and relevant interpretation of Winograd's view in the context of journalism would be that a robot journalist will not be able to "write" stories whose depth and richness will go beyond the "bureaucratic level", which may give an important advantage to human journalists who can express empathy and understand complex cultural contexts.

Indeed, the importance of NLP for the future of human journalism cannot be underestimated. NLP can help human and robot journalists cope to some extent with information overload by using NLP algorithms to automatically summarize long documents and extract new insights from huge data silos. Moreover, NLP algorithms can decipher the sentiment of texts in media and identify key communicators in social networks. By "combining the millions of tweets and other social media messages to determine how users feel about a particular product or service," NLP "has the potential to turn all of Twitter or Facebook into one giant focus group …" [Novoseltseva, 2017, para. 11]. Efficient NLP algorithms can be expected to be very useful for human journalists as they will allow them to discover new social trends as they emerge, based on actual social media conversations, which is a very important element in news stories.

10. AI Limitations: New Opportunities for Human Journalism

AI is based on a rational model, which implies that new information that does not reduce uncertainty "beyond the level of chance" is rejected by artificial neurons. The rational processes we have discussed above, however, place an upper limit to creativity at the transformational level of which a human is capable. Because AI algorithms cannot "think" out of the conceptual framework created for them by their human algorithm designers, they are unable of attaining the highest level of creativity that requires the ability to mentally cross into new unexpected conceptual frameworks.

The current limitations of AI, however, highlight the advantages of human journalists and create significant opportunities for them:

- AI algorithms cannot understand or express complex human emotions and social values in computational terms as necessary for analysis by AI algorithms.
- AI algorithms are limited in the level of creativity that they can generate, for several reasons. First, AI algorithms cannot simulate human brain processes that involve neurobiological chemical processes directly linked to human creativity. AI algorithms are confined to syntactic symbols that have no semantic meaning in themselves. Second, although AI algorithms operate primarily within the intelligence and knowledge expansion realm and can be expected to develop an "astronomical" IQ level, creativity is not directly related to IQ levels beyond a certain threshold. Third, high level human creativity and discovery are directly related to subconscious, intuition, dreaming, spontaneity, and emotional intelligence. All of these processes are also linked to "irrational thinking". AI algorithms developers are not as yet able to develop algorithms that include these very human capacities important to creativity. Fourth, creativity is often associated with human adventure and risk taking (which is also related to the human survival instinct). It will be very complex to program these human capabilities into an AI artificial brain.
- One of the most important functions of human journalism is to alert society to potential risks associated with environmental and social changes to the survival of the social system. AI algorithms can help humanity monitor, on a large scale, phenomena that may threaten humanity but such monitoring is performed within predefined indexes. AI algorithms cannot be expected to understand and monitor unexpected alarming developments: They lack the human capability to make connections not previously experienced. Moreover, AI algorithms will not alert society to potential evils of AI itself, or the potential physiological damage to the human brain due to the introduction of AI into all aspects of human lives. This is a major issue that future journalists must constantly research and address. Some early illustrations of such implications are found in work by Carr [2011, 2014] and Brynjolfsson and McAfee [2014], who demonstrate how AI and automation adversely affect human mental skills.
- AI algorithms are inherently influenced by the values and biases of their designers and scientists. It is the role of the future human journalists to understand the architectures of these algorithms and automatic processes and identify their shortcomings.
- Because the current level of Narrow AI algorithms have limited understanding of human natural language, especially the context of the ideas, metaphors, humor, and poetry, robot journalists are unable to "write" stories whose depth and richness go

beyond a "bureaucratic level". Such stories will necessarily be devoid of the empathy and understanding of complex cultural contexts, of which human journalists are capable.

- AI algorithms lack the ability to write opinions. They can produce new knowledge (after validation) but they cannot convert knowledge into policy proposals or suggestions for change.

Nonetheless, robot journalists pose an interesting challenge for human journalists. To compete with the robot journalists, the human journalists must "think different". They must learn to constantly look for new ways to tell a story. Human journalists must be familiar with scientific methods of analysis and must have a broad multidisciplinary education in the arts and philosophy, as a foundation for such searches for creative and innovative solutions. Furthermore, the human journalist must be thoroughly familiar with all the new digital tools available to them to efficiently data mine relevant data silos, and use AI tools as aids to help them generate new story formats. To this end, leading journalism schools, including the Columbia School of Journalism, are conducting "hackathons" to seek new ideas and to find new roles for human journalists in the age of smart algorithms. The word "hack" means a playful positive activity with the aim of creating new things or ideas in a restriction-free environment. On February 4, 2013, an Australian data journalism team from *The Age* conducted a hackathon involving programmers, data crunchers, journalists, graphic designers, and open data activists in Melbourne to "explore the relationship between big data to drive a narrative in the form of data visualization" [Wright, 2013, para. 1].

References

Andreasen, N. C. (2014). Secrets of the creative brain. *The Atlantic*. Retrieved from http://www.theatlantic.com/features/archive/2014/06/secrets-of-the-creative-brain/372299/

Boden, M. (1990). *The Creative Mind: Myths and Mechanisms* (2nd edn.). London and New York: Routledge.

Boden, M. (1998). Creativity and artificial intelligence. *Artificial Intelligence*, 103(1–2), 347–356.

Boden, M. (2009). Computer models of creativity. *AI Magazine*, 30(3), 23–34.

Brynjolfsson, E. and McAfee, A. (2014). *The second Machine Age: Work, Progress, and Prosperity in a Time of Brilliant Technologies*. New York: W. W. Norton & Company.

Cadwalladr, C. (2014). Are the robots about to rise? Google's new director of engineering thinks so ... *The Observer, Artificial Intelligence*. Retrieved from https://www.theguardian.com/technology/2014/feb/22/robots-google-ray-kurzweil-terminator-singularity-artificial-intelligence

Carr, N. (2011). *The Shallows: What the Internet is Doing to our Brains*. New York: W. W. Norton & Company.

Carr, N. (2014). *The Glass Cage: Automation and Us.* New York: W. W. Norton & Company.

Cope, D. (1996). *Experiments in Musical Intelligence with CD-ROM* (Computer Music and Digital Audio Series). Middleton, WI: A-R Editions.

Dickson, B. (2017). What is Narrow, General and Super AI. *Tech Talks.* Retrieved from https://bdtechtalks.com/2017/05/12/what-is-narrow-general-and-super-artificial-intelligence/

Eck, D. (2016). Welcome to Magenta. *Magenta.* Retrieved from https://magenta.tensorflow.org/welcome-to-magenta

Eder, D. (2003). What is singularity? BrainMeta.com Forum. Retrieved from http://brain-meta.com/forum/index.php?showtopic=1967

Frantz, R. (2003). Herbert Simon: Artificial intelligence as a framework for understanding intuition. *Journal of Economic Psychology*, 24, 266–277.

Gaskin, J. E. (2008). What ever happened to artificial intelligence? *Computerworld.* Retrieved from http://www.computerworld.com/article/2534413/business-intelligence/what-ever-happened-to-artificial-intelligence-.html

Hof, R. D. (2013). Deep learning. With massive amounts of computational power, machines can now recognize objects and translate speech in real time. Artificial intelligence is finally getting smart. *MIT Technology Review.* Retrieved from https://www.technologyreview.com/s/513696/deep-learning/

IBM Research. (2013). *Cognitive Environments.* Retrieved from http://researcher.ibm.com/researcher/view_group.php?id=5417

IBM Research. (2014). *Brain Power.* Retrieved from http://www.research.ibm.com/cognitive-computing/neurosynaptic-chips.shtml#fbid=Flx1v4VQ6Hm

Kahneman, D. (2017). *Remarks* [Video File]. NBER Conference Toronto: Economics of AI Conference. Toronto. Retrieved from https://digitopoly.org/2017/09/22/kahneman-on-ai-versus-humans/

Knight, W. (2017). The dark secret at the heart of AI. *MIT Technology Review.* Retrieved from https://www.technologyreview.com/s/604087/the-dark-secret-at-the-heart-of-ai/

Levy, S. (2013). How Ray Kurzweil will help Google make the ultimate AI brain. *Wired.* Retrieved from https://www.wired.com/2013/04/kurzweil-google-ai/

McCarthy, J., Minsky, M. L., Rochester, N., and Shannon, C. E. (1955). A proposal for the Dartmouth summer research project on artificial intelligence. Retrieved from https://www.cs.swarthmore.edu/~meeden/cs63/f11/AIproposal.pdf

Metz, R. (2017). Why Google's AI can write beautiful songs but still can't tell a joke. *MIT Technology Review.* Retrieved from https://www.technologyreview.com/s/608777/why-googles-ai-can-write-beautiful-songs-but-still-cant-tell-a-joke/

Moss, R. (2015). Creative AI: The robots that would be painters. *New Atlas.* Retrieved from http://newatlas.com/creative-ai-algorithmic-art-painting-fool-aaron/36106/

Novoseltseva, E. (2017). Natural language processing projects and startups to watch in 2017. *Apiumhub.* Retrieved from https://apiumhub.com/tech-blog-barcelona/natural-language-processing-projects/

Searle, J. (1990). Is the brain a mind computer program? *Scientific American*, 3(3), 417–458.

Searle, J. (2013). *Consciousness and the Brain* [Video file]. Retrieved from https://www.ted. com/talks/john_searle_our_shared_condition_consciousness

Simon, H. (1997). *Administrative Behavior* (4th edn.). New York: Free Press.

Smith, A. and Anderson, J. (2014). AI, robotics, and the future of jobs [Report]. *Pew Research Center, Internet & Technology*. Retrieved from http://www.pewinternet.org/2014/08/06/ future-of-jobs/

Somers, J. (2017). Is AI riding a one trick pony? *MIT Technology Review*. Retrieved from https://www.technologyreview.com/s/608911/is-ai-riding-a-one-trick-pony/

Stergiou, C. and Siganos, D. (2011). *Neural Networks*. Retrieved from https://www.doc. ic.ac.uk/~nd/surprise_96/journal/vol4/cs11/report.html

Trausan-Matu, S. (2005). Human language and the limits of artificial intelligence. A new religion-science relations. Paper presented at *Science and Religion: Global Perspectives*, Metanexus Institute, Philadelphia, PA. Retrieved from https://pdfs.semanticscholar.org/ ec25/98f2ba128f3f264a0b2b26ae5e2b57ccd6d2.pdf

Vinge, V. (1993). The coming technological singularity: How to survive in the post-human era. Paper presented at *Vision 21 Symposium* sponsored by NASA Lewis Research Center and the Ohio Aerospace Institute, March 30–31.

Winograd, T. (1991). Thinking machines: Can there be? Are we? In J. J. Sheehan and M. Sosna (Eds.), *The Boundaries of Humanity: Humans, Animals, Machines* (pp. 199–224). Berkeley: University California. Retrieved from http://publishing.cdlib.org/ ucpressebooks/view?docId=ft338nb20q&chunk.id=d0e4049&toc.depth=1&toc. id=d0e4049&brand=ucpress

Wright, G. (2013). Data flows at hackathon. *The Sydney Morning Herald*. Retrieved from http://www.smh.com.au/it-pro/blog/smoke-and-mirrors/data-flows-at-hackathon-20130207-2e2fn.html

Chapter 3

Robot journalism

Noam Lemelshtrich Latar

Automatic narration is emerging as a new field of research led by artificial intelligence (AI) software writers taking advantage of the vast body of knowledge in linguistics and the study of natural language. In automatic narration, AI algorithms are employed to automatically convert facts and new insights derived from data silos (also by AI tools) into readable stories, without human involvement, in a fraction of a second. Several commercial companies have already developed AI algorithms that write complete journalistic stories and adjust their tone and narrative structure to predefined audience profiles. It is estimated that within 5–10 years, the majority of all journalistic text stories will be written by robots. Welcome to the world of robotic journalism.

Through the practice of intensive and, at times, risky and expensive investigative journalism, traditional journalists aspire to reveal new facts and social trends. With their narrative talent, experience, values, creativity, and intuition, they convert these facts into journalistic stories for their audiences. The efficient new robot journalists may constitute strong competition for traditional journalists.

The new field of robotic journalism is based on two pillars: The computer software that automatically extracts new knowledge from huge data silos, and algorithms that automatically convert these insights and knowledge into readable stories without human involvement. Aside from great potential savings in labor costs, these robot journalists seldom miss facts, are never tired, and — if programmed objectively — are free of bias. The Japanese even created a 3D humanized robot journalist that can mingle in a crowd of people, conduct interviews, take pictures, and then compose a story [Lemelshtrich Latar, 2015].

Robotic journalism is viewed by some optimistic journalists as a tool that will release them from the necessity to conduct costly and, at times, dangerous investigations. Optimists hope that robot journalists will provide them with an automated draft for a story that human journalists will edit and enrich with their in-depth analysis, perspectives, and narrative talents. The more pessimistic journalists view new robot journalists as a genuine threat to their livelihood and style of working and living, especially in view of the anticipated pervasiveness of data-collecting micro-sensors embedded everywhere — in our clothing and in all the gadgets that surround us. Human journalists will be challenged to compete in this automatic comprehensive data collection and writing ecosystem.

These gloomy prophecies are not, however, inevitable. Due to several inherent limitations of AI algorithms, human journalists have some important advantages over robot journalists, but they must fully understand those limitations and adapt their mode of operation to take advantage of them.

1. Computational Journalism or Robotic Journalism

"... we define computational journalism as the combination of algorithms, data, and knowledge from the social sciences to supplement the accountability function of journalism" [Hamilton & Turner, 2009].

Computer assisted journalism, digital journalism, and robotic journalism describe different stages in the evolution in the integration of algorithms in journalism. According to Cox [2000], who offers a detailed history of the use of machines in journalism, the use of computers by journalists in newsrooms dates back to the early 1950s, coinciding with the early developments of the computer industry. Computer assisted journalism, also known as computer assisted reporting (CAR) [Karlsen and Stavelin, 2013], describes the early stage where computers were used mainly as a means to obtain research background while composing an article, pulling out statistics, and identifying similar stories that occurred in past years. Later, computers made it possible to retrieve information from digital libraries through the use of keywords in the search. Digital journalism mainly refers to the use of mining algorithms in search of hidden insights in huge data silos of structured and unstructured random data. An example of the use of digital journalism was published by Kira Radinsky, a data mining AI researcher, who applied data analytics tools to 150 years of articles from the NYT and other sources and discovered that in poverty areas if a year of drought is followed by a year of floods, there is a high probability of an eruption of a cholera epidemic. Her paper was published several months before the severe cholera epidemic in Cuba in 2012 that claimed many lives [Radinsky, 2012]. Robotic journalism describes the current stage in this evolution, in which algorithms are being employed for all the stages of journalistic work from information retrieval, through a search for hidden insights, and the automatic conversion of these insights into journalistic narratives, without human involvement.

Today, robot agents, robot editors, robot article generators, and — most recently — robot story writers are increasingly assuming roles that are traditionally associated with human journalists. Robot journalists may be comprised solely of computer software or embody a 3D structure or even humanoid appearance. Information-gathering robots such as the "Afghan Explorer" have also been used in war zones to survey areas in Afghanistan that are considered too dangerous for human journalists.

2. Robot Agents, Bots, and Virtual Assistants

Initially, the term "robots" was used in journalism to denote "robot agents" or "virtual assistants" that are able to "converse" with human journalists, mediating between them and the data silos. The term was coined by Lee and Kim [1998], who created the service "News On Demand" (NOD) in 1998, which used a robot to gather daily news information and deliver integrated newsfeeds to users. Subscribers to the service registered their information and received stories via email. Examples of these bots — essentially sophisticated AI algorithms — include **Wibbitz,** employed by *USA Today* to create short videos with narratives, and **News Tracer**, used by Reuters, whose algorithmic prediction tool helps journalists gauge the integrity of a tweet. The News Tracer bot scores emerging stories based on credibility and newsworthiness by evaluating who is tweeting about the story, how it is spreading across the network, and if nearby users have taken to Twitter to confirm or deny breaking developments [Keohane, 2017].

Another bot or virtual assistant is **BuzzBots,** an algorithm that collects information at news events. The algorithm was originally designed to crowdsource reporting from the Republican and Democratic National Conventions and is now used to collect information from on-the-ground sources at news events. BuzzBot has since been open-sourced, portending a wave of bot-aided reporting tools [Keohane, 2017].

Heliograf is an AI algorithm that *The Washington Post* employed in 2016 to make the newsroom an efficient environment for the journalists. According to Jeremy Gilbert, director of strategic initiatives at *The Post*, "The Heliograf software identifies the relevant data, matches it with the corresponding phrases in the template, merges them, and then publishes different versions across different platforms ..." The declared aim of the Heliograph is to "generate explanatory insightful articles ... to foster seamless intervention between human and machine." Heliograf was not intended to replace human reporters: It was designed as a "complementary service aimed at freeing up reporters and editors to cover more nuanced stories" [Mullin,

2016]. Most of all, Heliograf is designed to "grow its audience. Instead of targeting a big audience with a small number of labor-intensive human-written stories, Heliograf can target many small audiences with a huge number of automated stories about niche or local topics" [Keohane, 2017]. Robot writing algorithms are now in use by numerous media outlets: Bots are used by AP (to generate narratives on corporate earnings), Fox (to automatically generates sports news), and Yahoo (to create fantasy sports stories adjusted to its customers). Anyone can turn data into stories without writing a single line [Finley, 2015].

3. Robot Editors and Article Generators

One of the early uses of the term "robot journalism" was related to a robot editor developed by Google for its Google News Service. Google News, launched in 2002, is an aggregation service. Google developed an algorithm that "crawls" through thousands of news sites without human intervention and automatically selects the site's lead story and what is to be displayed on the home page, including the relevant links, based on a "source credibility" score. The product manager of the Google News Service boasted that "No team of human editors can compete with 24/7 robots" [Kurtz, 2002].

Google is currently working on a different type of robot editor. Jigsaw, a technology incubator that belongs to Google's parent company Alphabet, developed a new algorithmically driven application that separates toxic from non-toxic comments on publishers' websites. The "robot editor" evaluates comments based on their terminology, repetitive words, and level of aggression, and automatically assigns a score to the news items, reflecting its value. In general, the robot editor helps publishers and platforms to host better discussions online. *The New York Times* has partnered with Jigsaw to develop the editorial robot known as Perspective, which helps the newspaper increase the number of its stories open for comments, and frees up *The Times'* team of community editors who previously sorted through comments on 25% of all stories [Mullin, 2017].

4. Telepresence Mobile Robots and Mobile Robot Article Generators

In 2007, a Japanese team led by Matsumoto of the Department of Mechano-Informatics in the Graduate School of Information Science and Technology at the University of Tokyo engaged in the first and most ambitious endeavor to create a 3D robot journalist able to mingle in a crowd in a similar fashion to a human journalist. The algorithm developed by Matsumoto's group was programmed for "(1) autonomous exploration, (2) recording of news, and (3) generation of articles"

[Matsumoto *et al.*, 2007]. The Matsumoto robot was constructed on Segway wheels that provided mobility in a building or on a street. The robot was designed to explore the real world, take photos, transfer the information to a "news classifier" that calculated a "news score" based on an item's "anomaly" (scarcity) and "relevance". If the score was sufficiently high, the "article generator" produced an article.

The Beam is another mobile robot, developed by Suitable Technologies in Palo Alto, California. The Beam system is designed to enable the remote presence of a human journalist at an event, without anyone being physically there. The Beam facilitates multi-player mobile video conferences: Its motorized stand with a 17-inch flat screen can be remotely controlled by the user from a distance, allowing a person to have telepresence and conduct interviews in a manner similar to a video conference. The Beam system consists of a charging dock and a client software that connects the Beam to its operator over a network, allowing the Beam to move to various desired locations. The Beam enables interaction with other Beams that represent other users within the area.

Parmy Olson, a *Forbes* staff writer, visited the headquarters of Suitable Technologies, interviewed ST personnel, and wrote her journalistic story for *Forbes* on the telepresence robot producer, while remaining at home in San Francisco: "I'm exploring the headquarters of Suitable Technologies in Palo Alto, Calif., passing leather couches, paintings and large indoor plants. Only I'm not really here; I'm on a laptop at my desk in downtown San Francisco, roughly 30 miles away. Using some lightweight software, I'm controlling a Beam … that displays my face" [Olson, 2013]. Kashmir Hill, another *Forbes* staff writer, used Beam to visit the 2014 Consumer Electronics Show (CES). "All in all, it was a pretty nice way to check out the show without the headache of travelling there," wrote Hill [2014].

Another telepresence robot manufacturer is Double Robotics. According to its website, Double is "the ultimate tool for telecommuting. Double is a remotely controlled mobile teleconferencing system, enabling conversations to happen anywhere, anytime" (www.double robotics.com). Anybots, **another telepresence robot manufacturer, assigns an avatar to represent the journalist in the remote space.** "Short of being face-to-face, Anybots, Inc. offers the most interactive forms of communication available today by providing the user a personal remote avatar … With Anybots you can instantly be immersed in a distant environment experiencing the forefront of a new class of communication called mobile telepresence, allowing you to never miss an important event, meeting, or experience again" (www.anybots.com).

OhmniLabs is a robotics start-up whose telepresence mobile robot offers a unique tilting neck that allows Ohmni's operator to look up, down, and nod. With this single extra degree of freedom, Ohmni appears more connected to the person remotely inhabiting it, and conversations immediately assume a natural, comfortable quality, as the humans conversing with Ohmni feel less restricted, not forced to constantly aim at the device or sit in one spot. For journalistic work, conversations can continue longer and interviews can be conducted more conveniently, from any angle.

The telepresence robots do not, as yet, employ AI algorithms for their journalistic work, but will have an important impact on journalistic practice. As telepresence tools save travel time and expenses, their growing use can be expected to affect travel and tourism businesses. Moreover, the use of machines to replace physical contact will promote the acceptance of human-like journalist robots that replace human interaction. It won't be long before the AI features of the Japanese robot will be introduced into the next generation of telepresence robots replacing the Olsons and the Hills.

5. Robot Journalist Storywriters

A major change in the use of robotics in journalism occurred in 2010, when AI algorithms were developed in Northwestern University's computer science and communication labs with the objective of aiding human journalists in the very human occupation of writing stories. Narrative Science, a commercial company, grew out of the academic project in the labs. Narrative algorithms pioneers were careful to state that their objectives did not include totally replacing human journalists but merely to increase their efficiency. Following Narrative Science's footsteps, there are 12 automatic news narrative writing companies around the globe in the US, UK, Germany, Russia, China, and France. All of these companies develop robot journalists that perform data analysis and automatically write the narratives. Another major US leader in journalism robotics is Automated Insights.

6. Narrative Science

The first serious commercial attempt to convert facts into readable stories automatically was conducted at Northwestern University in a research project called the "Stats Monkey". The Stats Monkey algorithm was programmed to automatically generate baseball stories when fed game statistics. This research was led by Dr. Kristian Hammond and Dr. Larry Birnbaum, co-directors of the Intelligent Information Laboratory.

The Stats Monkey project evolved into the start-up Narrative Science in 2010 (www.narrativescience.com). With a multidisciplinary team of experts in computer science, communications, and business, Narrative Science developed and patented Quill, a new algorithm based on AI. The team's initial major objective was to implement a revolutionary approach to business analytics and natural language communication. Hammond, CTO of Narrative Science, was quoted as saying, "Quill's power lies in the fact that it is a synthesis of data analytics, artificial intelligence and editorial expertise" [Carter, 2013].

The Quill algorithm operates in three stages: data reception, extraction of key facts and insights from the data employing AI algorithms, and transformation of these facts and insights into readable stories without human involvement. Quill attempts to deliver both insights and predictions. Hammond explains, "The system uses the results of these analytics to drive a heuristically based inference engine and the central natural language generation. ... Give it data and Quill can reproduce a bonafide news story in seconds" [Carter, 2013]. According to Hammond, Quill is able to create a journalistic "spin" in addition to the stories [Marr, 2015]. Hammond claims that as NS grows, its stories will be able to provide explanatory journalism and, ultimately, long-form articles.

Quill allows NS customers to select the tone of the stories. "You can get anything, from something that sounds like a breathless financial reporter screaming from a trading floor to a dry sell-side researcher pedantically walking you through it," says Jonathan Morris, COO of Data Explorers, an NS customer [Levy, 2012]. "It's no more difficult to write an irreverent story than it is to write a straightforward, AP-style story," says Larry Adams, NS VP of Product [cited in Levy, 2012].

The Quill algorithm is programmed to learn the language of the domain it covers and write the stories in the appropriate language. For example, when Quill was assigned to write stories that cover the restaurant business in a given city, Quill was taught to learn the relevant components of a restaurant review, such as survey grades, service level, food experience, and citations from customers, using a database of restaurant reviews. In a short time, Quill could develop the narrative structure of the story and be able to write an endless supply of chirpy little restaurant reviews [Podolny, 2015]. Hammond predicts, "In 20 years, there will be no area in which Narrative Science doesn't write stories" [Levy, 2012].

Even the use of metaphors, a very human concept, is integrated into the Narrative Science algorithm. Hammond stated that Narrative Science is working to improve the quality of its articles by creating "deeper and better analytics, more expressiveness, more interesting parallelism and the use of metaphor" [Goldberg, 2013]. Nonetheless, Quill depends on data, and is therefore limited to writing stories only when data is available and questions are defined. Quill cannot initiate stories on its own without the data and a well-defined question.

As the pioneer of robot writing narratives, it may useful to focus on the predictions Narrative Science published for 2017 on its website: "NS predicts that conversational interfaces with the robots will become the norm. Designers of AI interfaces will add elements of tone, sentiment, timing, visual cues and word choices to the interaction and natural language will play a major role, all of which will make the algorithms much more accessible to the human journalists who are 'technophobes'."

NS predicts that efforts will focus on overcoming one of the most significant barriers in current AI systems: the inability of one AI system to interact with another AI system. Without such interactions and "universal standards for AI to AI interactions … AI technologies will increasingly become siloed or worse, interfere negatively with each other when multiple AI systems are involved in determining a single outcome" (https://narrativescience.com/Resources/Resource-Library/Article-Detail-Page/ 2017-predictions-for-artificial-intelligence-and-communication). Although integration among AI systems may take many years to develop, NS states that a major objective of AI research is to develop a "general AI system" that will allow separate "narrow AI" systems (that are currently unable to connect to or benefit from other AI systems that employ different algorithms) to "converse" with each other, to develop collective AI wisdom that resembles more how the human brain operates.

NS also predicts that efforts will be made to discover the biases of the algorithms. Today the algorithms that are being written are affected by the conscious or subconscious biases of the software writers. No tools are available as yet to search for these hidden biases, which are a major disadvantage of these robot writers.

Finally, NS believes that human journalism will come under the threat of media organizations that will compare the ROI (return on investment) on their human versus robotic journalists, which could lead to loss of human jobs and more risks to human journalist freedom of expression.

7. Automated Insights

Automated Insights, the other leading US (and global) robot journalism developer, claims that its patented AI algorithm is "like having your own personal data scientist, scouring large data sets and writing a story full of key insights for you. Except we do it in real time and at a scale of millions. … We are helping web site owners uncover the hidden insights in their web analytics. … We are publishing hundreds of millions of fully personalized stories … whether it is sports, finance, business intelligence — we can put any data in historical context in real time" (www.automatedinsights.com).

The Automated Insights algorithm can be programmed to write stories in any desired journalistic format: summaries, bullets, or long-form articles. Its real-time stories can be published on any scale in multiple formats — emails, mobile applications, and all types of social media. Customers of Automated Insights include Microsoft, Bloomberg, MSN, and *USA Today*.

The Automated Insights algorithms operate in a similar fashion to the NS algorithms: The technology "humanizes data" by identifying patterns and extracting key insights, derives and prioritizes insights based on the context and uniqueness, then constructs a narrative in any required format and language, and publishes the story using a cloud-based infrastructure in real time through all new media platforms (www.automatedinsights.com).

8. The Chinese Dreamwriter

The Chinese Internet giant Tencent entered robotic journalism narrative writing activities in 2015, when it introduced its Dreamwriter algorithm, equipped with high speed calculating and information searching ability, and the ability to write a new 1,000-word item in one minute. Tencent's aim was not to create a robot to replace human journalists, but to free human journalists to focus on more challenging and intelligent tasks [Can, 2015]. In the recent Brazil 2016 Olympic Games, Dreamwriter produced 450 Olympic news items over the 15-day sporting event, mostly about China's domination of the sports. The coverage was speedy, appearing minutes after events ended. Robot content writers are now also being embedded into electronic games, producing real-time stories based on how the users are performing during the games.

9. The Los Angeles Times

Ben Welsh, *LA Times* database manager, employs algorithms to create stories from the newspaper's database, which is automatically or manually fed by public or government authorities, such as the stock market results, the LAPD crime reports, and US Geological Survey (USGS) reports. When an earthquake of 3.2 magnitude shook California off the coast of San Simeon on February 1, 2013, the *LA Times* algorithm published the story within 8 minutes, complete with a map showing the epicenter of the quake. Journalist Ken Schwencke wrote the code that automatically composed and published the story [Marshall, 2013]. Ben Welsh explained, "The structured data comes in and Ken has an algorithm that says if the earthquake is close to California and over a certain magnitude it is 'news'. That automatically writes a blog post that looks like it was written by a human — well it was written by a human, by Ken — and it instantly creates a map, blog post, headline, and automatically posts it into our blogging platform." Ben Welsh views this auto-writing process as "human assisted reporting" [cited in Marshall, 2013, para. 7].

The *LA Times* algorithms are programmed to ask relevant questions that an experienced journalist would ask in a given situation. For example, in a crime story such as a homicide, the algorithm will search the database for who committed the most serious offense by looking at the highest bail amount, or comb through the list of occupations for public service jobs and familiar names [Marshall, 2013].

10. Conclusions

In 1942, science fiction author Isaac Asimov devised the following set of three rules to protect human beings from the potential dangers that robots pose to the human race:

(1) A robot may not injure a human being or, through inaction, allow a human being to come to harm.
(2) A robot must obey the orders given it by human beings except where such orders would conflict with the First Law.
(3) A robot must protect its own existence as long as such protection does not conflict with the First or Second Laws.

Asimov later added another law: "A robot must not harm humanity", called the "Zeroth Law", and emphasized that it preceded the other laws [Asimov, 1950].

When Asimov created his first set of Robot Laws, robots were assuming the roles of androids in science fiction writings, acting alongside human beings. However, current developments in AI aiming to emulate the human brain give a completely new meaning to the concept of robots, which is evident in robot journalism, where robots can and are replacing many functions of human journalists. These AI algorithms are coming dangerously close to violating the Zeroth Law because robots cannot effectively be programed to protect human rights and freedom of speech, which is crucial for social survival. This issue is elaborated in Chapter 10 on journalism and social goals.

Robot journalists are being developed at a rapid pace by commercial companies around the globe. These robots can be very efficient and quick, and operate at a very low cost. The quality of the narratives not only improves over time but the tone of the narrative can also be adjusted to fit various reader groups. These qualities create a considerable temptation for media organizations to replace their expensive, slow human journalists with efficient robots. With the recent global attack against the freedom of the press in Western democracies, coupled with a lack of public awareness of the important role of free journalism in protecting the interests of the public, these robots pose a huge threat to Western democracies and clearly violate Asimov's Zeroth Law ("A robot must not harm humanity"). Fortunately, these robots are limited to text narratives and are unable to create news stories that will be suitable to the changing media consumption habits of generations Y and Z. These new media consumption habits require fewer texts and more emphasis on integrating video clips, new technologies like VR and AR, and new interactive applications. These are discussed in Chapter 6 in this book.

References

Asimov, I. (1950). *I Robot*. New York: Doubleday & Company.

Can, Y. (2015). China's Tencent Develops a Robot Journalist to Write News Stories. *People's Daily Online*. Retrieved from http://en.people.cn/n/2015/0911/c90000-8949019.html

Carter, J. (2013). Could robots be the writers of the future? *Techradar.com*. Retrieved from http://www.techradar.com/news/computing/could-robots-be-the-writers-of-the-future-1141399

Cox, M. (2000). *The Development of Computer Assisted Reporting*. Paper presented at the Newspaper Division, Association for Education in Journalism and Mass Communication, Southeast Colloquium, University of North Carolina, Chapel Hill.

Finley, K. (2015). This news-writing bot is now free for everyone. *Wired*. Retrieved from https://www.wired.com/2015/10/this-news-writing-bot-is-now-free-for-everyone/

Goldberg, S. (2013). Robot writers and the digital age. *American Journalism Review*. Retrieved from http://ajr.org/2013/11/25/computer-might-replace-robot-journalism-digital-age/

Hamilton, J. T., and Turner, F. (2009). Accountability through algorithm: Developing the field of computational journalism. A report from *Developing the Field of Computational Journalism*, a Center for Advanced Study in the Behavioral Sciences Summer Workshop, Stanford, CA.

Hill, K. (2014). I, Robot journalist: Beaming into CES 2014 from my kitchen. *Forbes Online*. Retrieved from https://www.forbes.com/sites/kashmirhill/2014/01/08/i-robot-journalist-beaming-into-ces-from-my-kitchen/#5d4f5dba7fb1

Karlsen, J. and Stavelin, E. (2013). Computational journalism in Norwegian newsrooms. *Journalism Practice*, 8(1). doi.org/10.1080/17512786.2013.813190.

Keohane, J. (2017). "What news-writing bots mean for the future of journalism." *Wired*. Retrieved from https://www.wired.com/2017/02/robots-wrote-this-story/

Kurtz, H. (2002). Robotic journalism: Google Introduces human-less news. *Washington Post*. Retrieved from http://andrewcoile.com/CSUMB/2002/fall/CST373/scrapbook/robot journalism.pdf

Lee, S. M. and Kim, T. Y. (1998). A news on demand service system based on robot agent. *Proceedings of the 1998 International Conference on Parallel and Distributed Systems* (pp. 528–532). Taiwan, ROC, December 14–16, 1998. Washington DC: IEEE Computer Society.

Lemelshtrich Latar, N. (2015). The robot journalist in the age of social physics. In G. Einav (Ed.), *The New World of Transitioned Media* (pp. 65–80). Springer. doi: 10.1007/978-3-319-09009-2.

Levy, S. (2012). Can an algorithm write a better news story than a human reporter? *Wired*. Retrieved from https://www.wired.com/2012/04/can-an-algorithm-write-a-better-news-story-than-a-human-reporter/

Marr, B. (2015). *Can Big Data Algorithms Tell Better Stories than Humans?* Retrieved from https://www.forbes.com/sites/bernardmarr/2015/07/22/can-big-data-algorithms-tell-better-stories-than-humans/#3939d0ee14b5

Marshall, S. (2013). Robot reporters: A look at the computers writing the news. *Journalism. co.uk*. Retrieved from https://www.journalism.co.uk/news/robot-reporters-how-computers-are-writing-la-times-articles/s2/a552359/

Matsumoto, R., Nakayama, H., Harada, T., and Kuniyoshi, Y. (2007). Journalist robot: Robot system making news articles from real world. *Proceedings of the 2007 IEEE/RSJ, International Conference on Intelligent Robots and Systems*, San Diego, CA.

Mullin, B. (2016). The Washington Post will use automation to help cover elections. *Poynter*. Retrieved from http://www.poynter.org/2016/the-washington-post-will-use-automation-to-help-cover-the-election/435297/

Mullin, B. (2017). The New York Times is teaming up with Alphabet's Jigsaw to expand its comments. *Poynter*. Retrieved from http://www.poynter.org/2017/the-new-york-times-is-teaming-up-with-googles-jigsaw-to-expand-its-comments/463135/

Olson, P. (2013). Rise of the telepresence robots. *Forbes Online*. Retrieved from https://www.forbes.com/sites/parmyolson/2013/06/27/rise-of-the-telepresence-robots/#e6ff 20bac034

Podolny, S. (2015). If an algorithm wrote this, how would you even know? *The New York Times*. Retrieved from https://www.nytimes.com/2015/03/08/opinion/sunday/if-an-algorithm-wrote-this-how-would-you-even-know.html

Radinsky, K. (2012). *Learning to Predict the Future using Web Knowledge and Dynamics*. (Unpublished doctoral dissertation). Computer Science Department, Technion, Israel. Retrieved from http://www.cs.technion.ac.il/users/wwwb/cgi-bin/tr-get.cgi/2013/PHD/ PHD-2013-02.pdf

Chapter 4

Big data and advanced analytics

Amir Ruskin

1. The Moment of Birth of Big Data and Analytics

If anything comes close to the impact of the two earlier seminal moments in the story of man — recorded history and the printing press — it is Big Data and Analytics. At no point in history has it ever been so easy to create, record, analyze, and be impacted by data. How did we come to amass such huge amounts of data? Because of two things — our fascination with data and the ease of data collection, facilitated by social networks and the Internet of Things (IoT).

In this chapter, we will guide you on a journey through the amazing eco-system that is the digital universe. From the promise of Big Data and the fundamental methods of data analysis used to make sense of data, to the eruption of cloud services that propel opportunities in fast-forward mode, we will see how data have created a game changer. From there, we will offer a window to the stories that data can tell, especially when powered by advanced analytics such as Data Science, Machine Learning, Artificial Intelligence (AI), and many other ultra-sophisticated means of data analysis. We will conclude by explaining how the data economy is currently evolving from a data-as-a-service model to data-as-a-product model.

Human beings have always been fascinated by data. We've been curious about questions ranging from why people were dying of the Bubonic plague in Europe, to how people survived the Great Depression. But these questions always required slow, manual collection of layers upon layers of data, going from door to door, asking people questions, and collating their responses. When some modicum of sense could be made of the findings, much water had flowed under the bridge, making this compilation dated and of little use. Today, the IoT, the network of devices connected by the Internet, makes it possible to amass and share large amounts of data, including the minutest details, in a short span of time. Perhaps it's easier to explain what Big Data can do, instead of trying to define it, because there are many definitions of Big Data flying around. For me, Big Data is the massive quantities of data that are produced by digital processes, and our actions on social media that, when harnessed, analyzed, and applied, can give you a competitive edge, no matter what your profession.

Big Data is also a boon to journalists: There is a lot that journalists and the media can do to harness the power of data and technology in order to create added value for journalism. For example, understanding the SoLoMo (Social, Local, and Mobile) principle, which is used by marketers to target customers, is of great assistance to journalists too. SoLoMo pivots on information about people's uses of personalized sites and applications, especially social networks: Information on what they posted on Facebook, where they checked in, what they liked and shared on Instagram, their location and how they use their mobile phone. The resulting data collected about any single user can be used by a newspaper, news website, or a magazine, to produce and direct, or target, specific articles to that individual on the basis of his/her likes and preferences, enhancing the relevance of the information to the reader, and increasing consumer loyalty: As a result of the fit between reader and content, the reader will return to the newspaper, magazine, or website for more information.

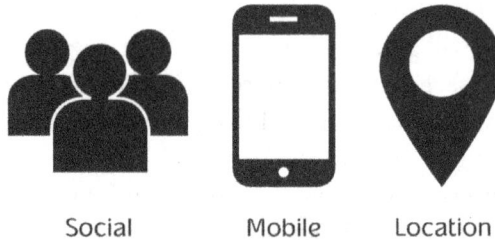

Social   Mobile   Location

In another example of how data analytics is being used to create new media value, media organizations are already training machines to publish stories immediately after an event becomes known, with the help of algorithms that mine crucial bits of data and cobble together a breaking news headline. But, Big Data's biggest value is the predictive powers that it gives a journalist. When used and analyzed correctly, Big Data can predict wars and labor strikes, terror attacks, election results, and online spending (see Figure 1) and help journalists tip readers off in advance to changing fashion trends, natural disasters, traffic jams, crop patterns, and much more. Using Big Data, data-hungry journalists can apply the full force of the digital devices and data-receptor sensors at their disposal to the data they collect, not only to publish news but to make predictions that offer potential benefits to their readers.

Bra size and online spending power

	Low	Slightly low	Middle	Slightly high	high
B	0%	65%	28%	7%	0%
C	1	21	61	12	5
E	0.7	14	61	18	6
D	1.2	13	53	26	7

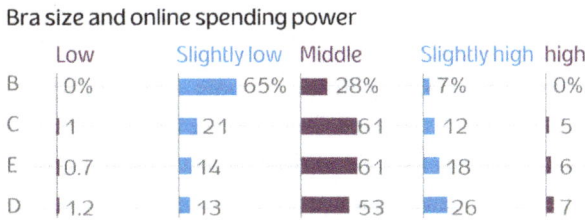

Figure 1.   Using bra size to predict online shopping habits.

Source: https://qz.com/295370/how-alibaba-is-using-bra-sizes-to-predict-online-shopping-habits/.

SalesPredict, acquired by eBay in July 2016, is a good example of the already available power of prediction in large-scale data sets and high-volume usage intensity. "The acquisition will support eBay's Artificial Intelligence, Machine Learning and Data Science efforts to support its structured data plan. ... or our buyers, it will help us better understand the price differentiating attributes of our products, and, for our sellers, it will help us build out the predictive models that can define the probability of selling a given product, at a given price over time" (https://www.ebayinc.com/stories/news/ebay-acquires-salespredict).

On Google Cloud Platform, you can find a simple tool that helps predict future financial market events based on real-life public data from Quandl (which advertises itself as "the premier source for financial, economic, and alternative datasets, serving investment professionals") (https://cloud.google.com/solutions/machine-learning-with-financial-time-series-data).

Kaggle.com periodically sponsors interesting competitions in data analytics (Data Science) with some of the world's most challenging analytical questions. Recently, the world's best data scientists were challenged to help the Department of Homeland Security improve the accuracy of the algorithms that it uses to predict passenger threats, offering a USD 1.5 million reward for the best algorithm (https://www.kaggle.com/c/passenger-screening-algorithm-challenge).

---

2. How Are Data Analyzed?

To understand data analytics, we must first understand the digital universe, in which every object has multiple aspects. Let's take the example of all the people who attended a music festival that was the target of a terrorist attack. The data on the people at this event can be compiled on the basis of race, income group, gender, educational background, or other categories. Race, income, gender, and educational background become aspects that are analyzed by slicing, dicing, and drilling each (or a combination of them) to break down data into smaller parts or examine the information from different perspectives in order to enhance our understanding (slicing implies cutting into a part of the data before dicing it further into smaller bits, while drilling down its dividing information in thin layers in a hierarchical manner). The amount of data available on a single event is tremendous. Even if a journalist using traditional methods to seek information limits their search to the demographics of people who attended the concert, the task would still be like looking for a needle in a haystack. Data analysis technologies can do this in seconds, with the ultimate aim of presenting findings in segments that are comprehensible to humans.

Since the dawn of civilization, humans have been capable of seeing only two or three dimensions (as the visual universe is perceived by us). Therefore, visualization and infographics can further break down the topic into many more insightful and easy to understand segments. When you see how data from one event can be analyzed on multiple dimensions, you begin to understand the possibilities of data analysis, and its value, not only for journalists but for anyone who can benefit from the depth of information.

Many media organizations are already using data analytics to increase customer engagement, grow readership, and increase the efficiency of newsroom operations. For example, infographics has become a new appealing mode of repackaging and consuming news; The infographic trend is backed by statistics that show that visuals and infographics are read more than text. Every media organization's requirements and goals are different and hence the analytic tools and methods they use also differ, as are the new organizational functions that media organizations establish to utilize data: audience engagement editors, audience development editors, and chief data officers. All are experts who work with traditional journalists to make their work more data informed, and ensure that data analytics are used efficiently and effectively.

3. Data and the Cloud Revolution

In the past, newsrooms and media organizations were the repositories of data, news, and information collated on the world's major events over the years; but today, with unimaginable amounts of data being created every nanosecond, we have a problem of plenty. The amount of data in the digital universe far exceeds the storage capacity of the average corporation's data center. Technology created this problem of plenty, but it also created the solution: Today, third parties offer to host data on their servers (known as public or private cloud services), creating easy access to and sharing of the data stored on any of the thousands of available cloud-based platforms, from anywhere. The simplest example of a cloud storage service is an email server that saves an individual's emails, which can be accessed from any device, anywhere in the world.

Big Data and cloud storage and computing go hand-in-hand. They are interconnected and interdependent. The more we use devices and social media, the more data that are created, refined, and analyzed, and stored in data warehouses — and the more we have the power to predict customer behaviors, choices, and interests on the basis of past preferences.

Big Data management software such as Hadoop helps us analyze data and retarget it to provide personalized and customized news to readers and consumers of media products. Until now, we have been able to analyze finite sets of data, but the most exciting development in technology is the new ability to analyze data in real time, as they are being collected from cell towers and switches. These real-time analytical capabilities give media professionals, especially those who report on critical issues as they develop, the added value of complementing their live reports with mint-fresh data that has just been collected, processed, and analyzed. Journalists no longer need to wait for investigation results to bolster their reporting: Instead, they can access data easily from cloud-based platforms in real time. How the full force of this development will impact media professionals (the consumers of this service) can only be imagined, although it will definitely add a predictive dimension to news reporting. With the power to predict readers' preferences, highly personalized stories targeted at the most relevant audience will become possible.

Another good example of free business intelligence (BI) tools you can easily install and use with minimal technical knowledge is the BIRT open source project (http://www. eclipse.org/birt). The following screenshot is of a sample report anyone can generate from their own data:

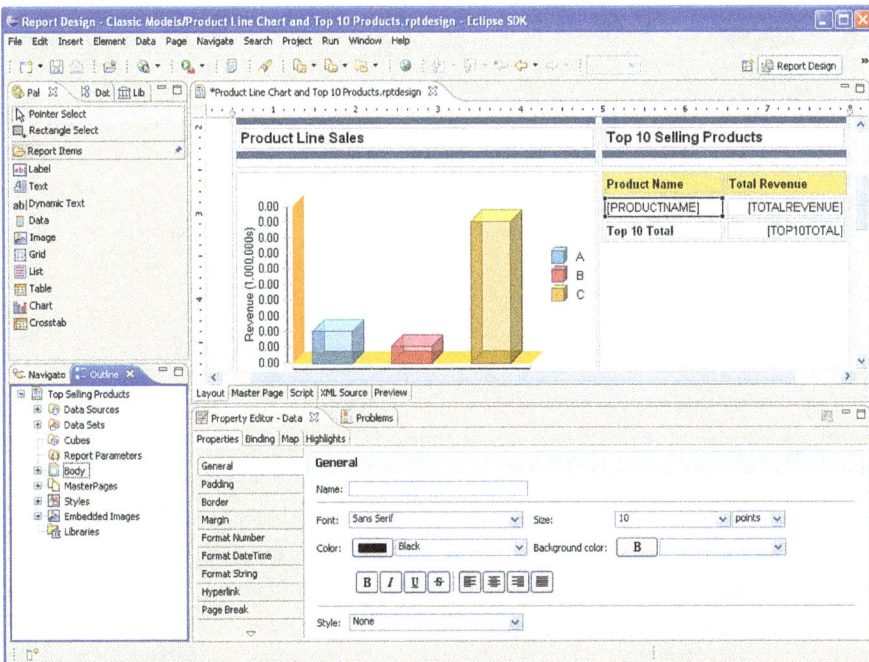

Most prime data technology companies offer cloud-based solutions that can be used directly. For example, Amazon's AMS (Amazon Web Services) can be used to easily start and run a Big Data application. You can actually set up an environment, even for personal use, and begin analyzing large-scale data sets that you receive or purchase. See https://aws.amazon.com/big-data/getting-started.

The "personal" version of ClicData, which focuses on an easy-to-analyze capabilities and great outcomes, including graphics:

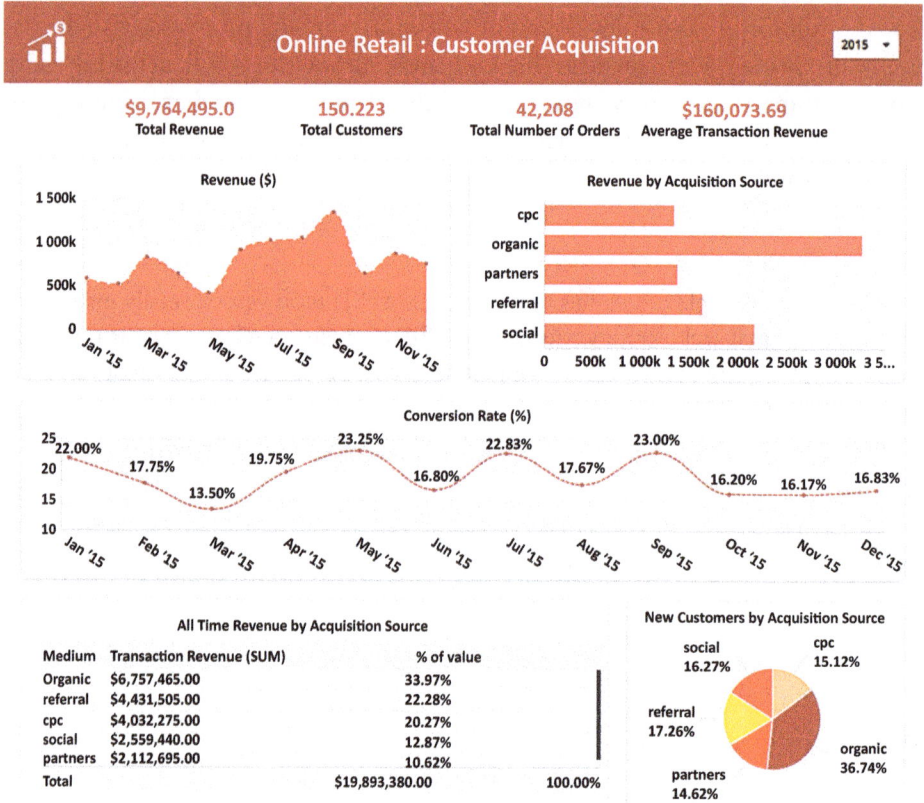

http://www.clicdata.com/pricing/personal.

Huge amounts of data can be found, and initially even queried directly in many Open Data initiatives currently managed by world governments. For example, many US Bureau of Labor statistics, such as inflation and prices, employment and unemployment, pay and benefits, and much more, are available on its website.

The most straight-forward tool to try slicing-and-dicing information is Microsoft Excel's Pivot Table capability. Load into your Excel any multi-dimensional data set. For example, in the USA Data.gov public site, you can find New York State University Construction Fund contracts since 1995, in a CSV format that is easily loaded into your Excel. Apply the Pivot table functionality under Insert/PivotTable — you'll be surprised how much you can achieve by yourself (https://catalog.data.gov/dataset/state-university-construction-fund-sucf-contracts-beginning-1995).

In the public Indie Web (a people-focused initiative and alternative to the "corporate web") social graph and dataset of its activity are available. You can find data analysis and great interactive data visualizations at http://www.indiemap.org:

Indie Map Statistics

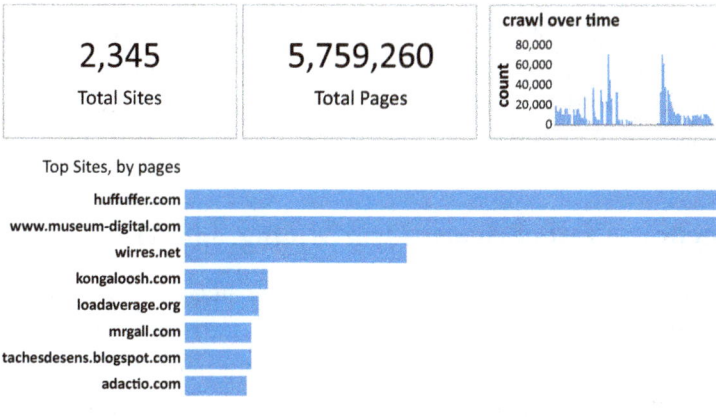

2,345	5,759,260	crawl over time
Total Sites	Total Pages	

Top Sites, by pages

- huffuffer.com
- www.museum-digital.com
- wirres.net
- kongaloosh.com
- loadaverage.org
- mrgall.com
- tachesdesens.blogspot.com
- adactio.com

Explore the Madison Initiative, aimed to "help create the conditions in which the US Congress and its members can deliberate, negotiate and compromise in ways that work for most Americans." The data are queried using Kumu, "a powerful data visualization platform that helps you organize complex information into interactive relationship maps" [http://kumu.io]. This cloud-based solution that requires no software installations promises that users with no technical background will be "up and running" in seconds.

4. Data Tell a Story

We're all heading toward a data-driven, data-optimized economy. Machines will look for patterns and train themselves to solve problems and make predictions. AI — when machines mimic human minds — will soon be generating data from machines: a golf club will give feedback on your swing or a washing machine will tell you how long it will take to clean a load of laundry. In the expectation that media consumers will subscribe to knowledge in the form of data products, media organizations have already started using Data Science to build in-house products that interpret and predict customer behavior. Machines can be trained to predict when consumer interest is dropping, whether certain kinds of stories are doing well, and when positive stories work better than negative ones. In-house data scientists in media organizations such as *The New York Times* are making sense of data, training machines to see patterns and make predictions, in hope of reaping the benefits of Machine Learning and AI to bolster bottom lines.

The newsroom is at a cross roads. Old learnings and practices are no longer able to sustain interest when information is not the sole prerogative of traditional media. Just as we now use Google maps to find our way around, news will be consumed on the basis of how it impacts our needs for information and knowledge. In an excellent article published in the *Harvard Business Review*, Strikeleather [2013] outlines the main steps to a great data story: create a compelling narrative, tailor it to the audience, maintain objectivity and balance, and don't drop data that don't fit your narrative. We would add — become fluent in data language and its tools. It is undoubtedly the next language that journalists should master.

5. Advanced Analytics — Data Science, Data Mining, and AI

In today's information economy, every act we perform leaves huge data traces in our wake, and these are all collected, processed, and analyzed. Extracting information from these sources, the first and most crucial step to building piles of data, is what advanced analytics is about. The insights and information can be ploughed back into the various organizations to see how their work can have more impact or be made more efficient on the basis of the data analyses.

For every journalist or media person, the starting point of a story is a simple "Why?". While many ordinary people may be satisfied with an answer to just one "why" question, a journalist's questions never stop: The need to dig deeper and get to the bottom of the truth is the journalist's unending quest. Frequently, the process of investigative journalism begins with a hunch, when a journalist notices that something is not quite right: Data are then sought, collected, and analyzed. In contrast, with advanced analytics, machines can be trained to look for patterns in data, analyze them quickly, and generate insights that the journalist can then use to develop a narrative, without waiting to develop a hunch.

AI and Machine Learning are two other terms that are hot talking points today. Everyone throws these terms into their talk. The two terms are frequently used interchangeably and quite understandably so, because they feed off of each other. AI refers to the ability of systems and devices to behave and act intelligently and independently.

For example, news agencies have partnered with third party AI technology providers to issue automatically drafted quarterly business reports or sports reports. The use of AI has resulted in 10 times more reports being generated, with fewer errors, yet there are limited opportunities to create such automated reports because the use of the technology is not widespread.

News agency Reuters partnered with semantic technology company Graphiq to produce interactive data visualizations that can be used with news reports generated by Reuters' staff. These interactive data visualizations are produced and updated constantly, depending on how a story might develop. Much richer than an archive of photos, the visualizations are constantly being updated in real time, as data come in. However, AI applications are still in their infancy and all is not rosy in this realm. When Facebook experimented with AI to curate its Trending Topics, it suffered embarrassment and was forced to remove one of the curated stories that was discovered to be a fake story — a telling reminder that AI cannot be left to function unmonitored, not yet.

The AI revolution is powered by Machine Learning. After so many years in which engineers tried to design machines to do something, today, the focus is on letting machines learn to do things on their own. Engineers have stopped coding directly, and instead, teach computers and machines to identify patterns and processes. They connect these learning machines to the Internet, give them access to data, and sit back as the machines analyze and act on them. For example, newspapers can employ Machine Learning to analyze readers' feedback on stories they liked and didn't like, and then identify stories that might interest a certain category of readers.

See the eye-opener analysis generated by *The Huffington Post* on the topics that interested its visitors. The ability to analyze massive data and generate predictions (i.e., the issues HuffPost visitors will be interested in) or classifications (i.e., how to classify visitors into groups that act similarly) are the exclusive domain of Data Science analysis. See http://reutersinstitute.politics.ox.ac.uk/publication/big-data-media.

6. Analytics as a Service

All media organizations have a lot to benefit from the vast amount of data available, but to do so, and to remain competitive, they must employ new, sophisticated data-related technologies. Major media organizations such as *The New York Times* have set up departments that are transitioning the organizations into digital companies. Others, like news agency Reuters, are partnering with third parties to fill this gap in the fast-evolving journalism market.

These are two examples of how companies are working with today's data technology. One directly recruits its own team of data scientists while the second has opted to work with an external automated interactive graphics provider with expertise in data visualization. The latter is an example of using analytics as a service, where a media organization outsources its analytical capacity for a fee. Instead of setting up an entire digital eco-system within one's organization, an organization can commission analytics as a service, for some of its data analysis needs (called a hybrid system) or all of them, effectively allowing the organization to focus on its core competency.

Analytics as a service is rapidly gaining ground, and a growing number of companies with expertise in analytics are offering this now vital service, off-site. In fact, data scientists are one of the most highly sought-after professionals in the world and analytics-as-a-service models range from consulting agencies, on-site installation, or via crowdsourcing. Many solutions have reached maturity and can provide complete project development, management, and operating services from remote locations including India, Estonia, and China.

7. Data as a Product — Data Monetization

Like money, data can reveal its true worth only when put to the best possible use. You might have a million terabytes of data and more coming in every second, but the real value of the data is reflected in what you choose to do with it. Since data is the definitive game changer in the digital world, those who use it well will have a competitive edge over others.

Some pioneering businesses have already started maximizing data's economic potential by identifying an opportunity and then trying to see how the data at their disposal can be used to solve it, rather than the other way around. For example, let's say that a media organization is looking to retain its readers. Data that the company has about its readers can be analyzed on the basis of several variables, such as spending power, income bracket, relevance of content, and age group, in order to classify and then deliver the data that readers want. This type of data analysis can be performed in-house or outsourced to a service provider.

To make products more appealing, media organizations are always looking to produce, package, and bundle content in different ways. Entertainment-on-demand and pay-per-view have become well-established options. Certain media organizations are giving their customers the choice of buying their favorite programs, establishing payment gateways with third party providers, and constantly looking for new ways of revenue generation.

The data that media organizations accumulate can be sold as raw or processed data, and analyzed to discover correlations and generate insights, and leverage this information in transactions with business partners. Data that media organizations gather may serve them well as they seek to glean more information about their readers and retarget them in their strategies by partnering with third parties including mobile service providers, credit card companies, and companies that advertise on their platforms.

Many technologies have been created and commercialized around data monetization. DMPs (Data Management Platforms) are emerging while many of the most powerful enterprises in the marketing and technology arena are gaining market coverage and power. DMPs are new creatures. They are "central hubs that store and analyze all of a company's customer, audience, and marketing data. DMPs help companies make best use of the massive amounts of data they collect by analyzing data from multiple sources and presenting it in easily digestible ways. DMPs are used by ad agencies, marketers, and publishers to create rich, custom data sets and more effectively target users for online advertising" (G2Crowd site). DMPs are the new stock exchanges bourses for data monetization in the marketing arena, and are obviously only one example of the potential of data monetization. See Figure 2 for the major players in this field, based on a G2 Crowd Grid.

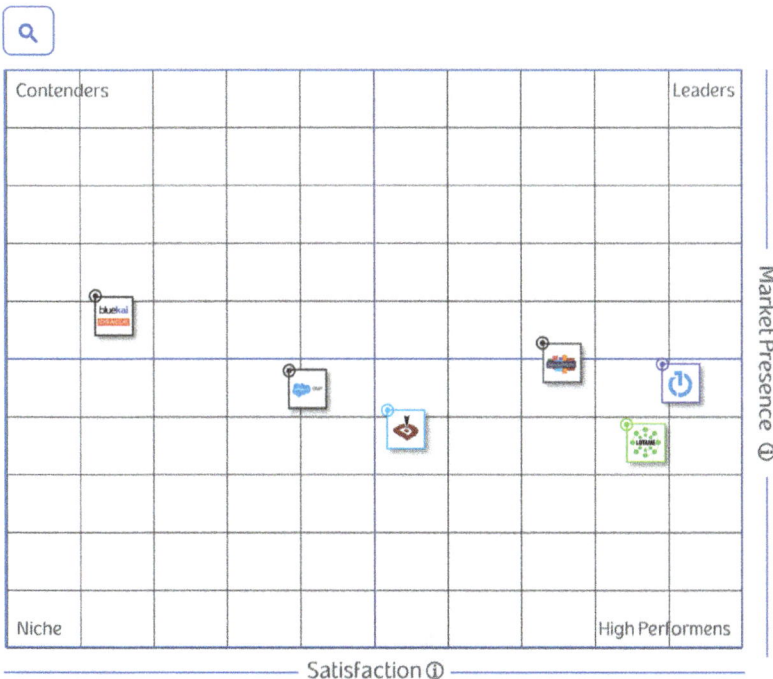

Figure 2.   Major Data Management Platforms (DPMs).

Source: https://www.g2crowd.com/categories/data-management-platform-dmp.

While we're still a long way from understanding the full potential of Big Data and its impact, it's important to know that our understanding of data is evolving. While we are still trying to wrap our heads around issues such as privacy and security, it's clear that Big Data will have far-reaching effects on the way we consume media and how media will make itself more relevant and personal, how it will mesh better with our preferences, and be a valuable source of information to many of its existing and new business partners.

Reference

Strikeleather, J. (2013). How to tell a story with data. *Harvard Business Review*. Retrieved from https://hbr.org/2013/04/how-to-tell-a-story-with-data

Chapter 5

Automatic newsrooms

Noam Lemelshtrich Latar

Automatic processes employing AI algorithms are penetrating all aspects of news production and dissemination: All forms of news content are being automatically tagged for efficient subsequent news searches; Algorithms search for new insights in huge data silos and automatically compose narratives without human involvement; and finally, AI engines target the news per the consumers' digital profiles. There are predictions that these automatic processes will lead to fully automated news rooms without human journalists.

1. Automated Newsrooms

Media companies are expected to undergo dramatic changes in the coming decade due to the introduction of automated AI processes into all aspects of news production and dissemination. In the pursuit of efficiency, media organizations (possibly with the exception of public media) can be expected to increase their investments in automation, the creation of data silos, and the construction of AI algorithms that can data-mine new facts and social trends, write the stories, and automatically target the content to the appropriate consumers in the relevant media consumption context. AI algorithms will be employed to perform automated content analysis and tagging in all types of media content (text, video, audio, and images), analysis and tagging of the contextual aspects of media consumption, including social setting, location, program mood, and consumers' mood and engagement during content consumption [Lemelshtrich Latar and Nordfors, 2009]. By creating comprehensive social DNAs of consumers, these AI algorithms allow media organizations to automatically select and transmit content and advertising that match consumers' digital profiles [Lemelshtrich Latar, 2004].

The ability to accurately measure content's effect on both consumer behavior and individual journalists' ROI can be expected to exert tremendous pressure on journalists to adjust content according to the revenues that each of their articles generate for the media organization. Robot journalists will be programed to do exactly that, automatically. Their speed of work and the ability to automatically send content directly to consumers based on their profiles give robot journalism a significant advantage in the competition for consumer attention and dollars, and pose a genuine threat for human journalists.

These new automated newsrooms can be expected to be run by new leaders such as data silo managers and software writing engineers. When asked what he would do in his media organization, given his experience, Arthur Sulzberger, publisher of *The New York Times*, said, "Hire more engineers" [Doctor, 2013].

2. Behavioral Targeting

Behavioral targeting is the term given to a technique employed by commercial or political content providers to adjust content units to consumers' digital profiles, in order to significantly increase the impact of the content on consumers' commercial or political behavior. Behavioral targeting is made possible by AI engines that allow content providers and website owners to continuously monitor their consumers' web behavior and use this information to construct personal digital profiles. AI algorithms can "deliver ads to consumers based on their behavior while viewing web pages, shopping on-line for products and services, typing keywords into search engines or combinations of all three ..." [Williamson, 2005].

The behavioral-targeting AI model described in Figure 1 outlines the basic information-flow elements that automatically analyze journalistic content on all platforms and transmit relevant content and advertisements to consumers according to their digital identities. Journalistic content is monitored constantly as consumers interact and make choices — and this information is fed into the dynamic learning model that is constantly updated as it "learns" consumers' profiles and content preferences and continuously improves the accuracy of these profiles. The AI engine also monitors contextual parameters and consumers' emotional states during interaction or consumption by analyzing consumers' verbal or other responses. A brief description of the information flow illustrates the process:

- **Step One:** All journalistic content is analyzed by smart AI algorithms and automatically annotated (tagged);

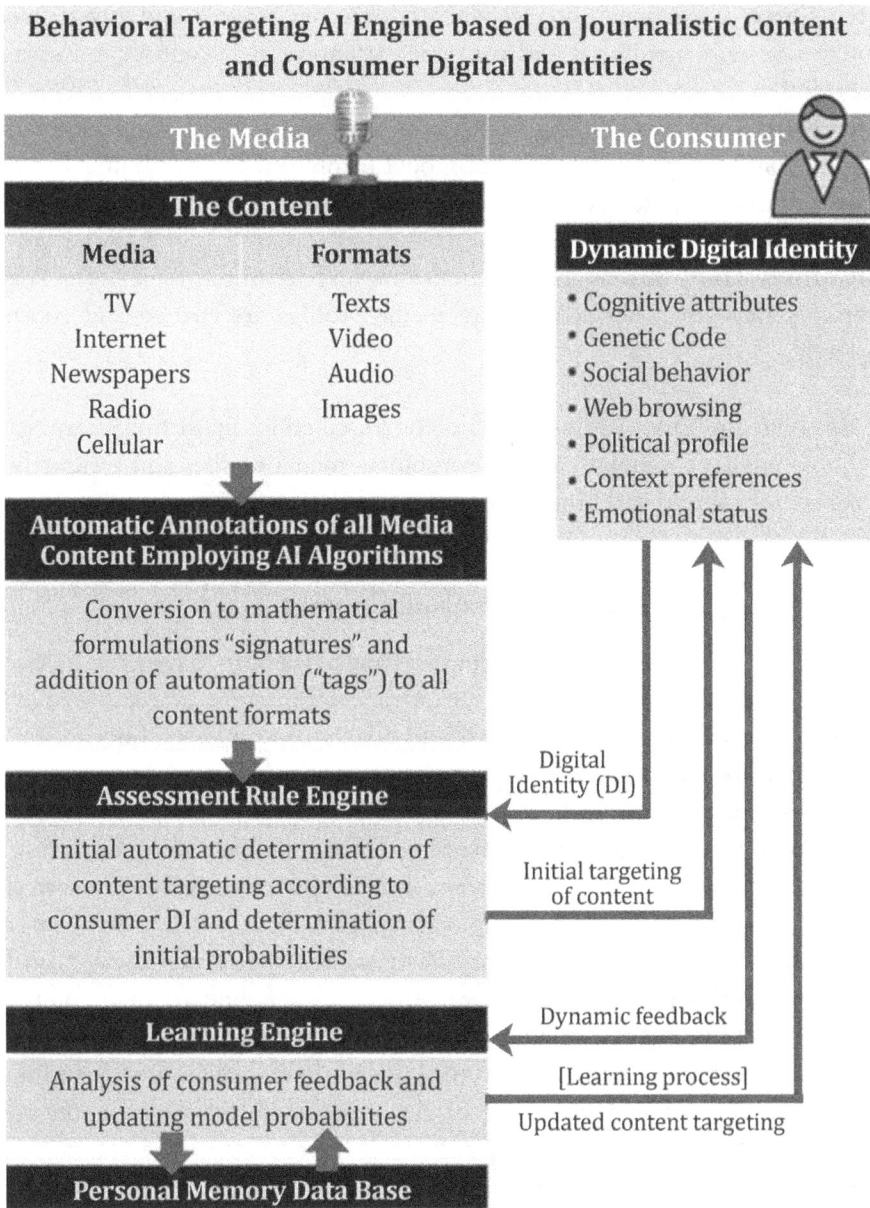

Behavioral Targeting AI Engine based on Journalistic Content and Consumer Digital Identities

The Media

The Consumer

The Content

Media	Formats
TV	Texts
Internet	Video
Newspapers	Audio
Radio	Images
Cellular	

Dynamic Digital Identity
- Cognitive attributes
- Genetic Code
- Social behavior
- Web browsing
- Political profile
- Context preferences
- Emotional status

Automatic Annotations of all Media Content Employing AI Algorithms

Conversion to mathematical formulations "signatures" and addition of automation ("tags") to all content formats

Assessment Rule Engine

Initial automatic determination of content targeting according to consumer DI and determination of initial probabilities

Digital Identity (DI)

Initial targeting of content

Learning Engine

Analysis of consumer feedback and updating model probabilities

Dynamic feedback

[Learning process]

Updated content targeting

Personal Memory Data Base

Figure 1.   Model of a behavioral targeting AI engine.
Source: Lemelshtrich Latar and Nordfors, 2009.

- **Step Two:** Consumers' digital identities and annotated content are fed to the Assessment Rule Engine for initial content determination. Relevant ads are sent to consumers based on their profiles;

- **Step Three:** Consumers interact with the selected content and advertisements. Interactions are monitored and consumer attention and feedback are measured constantly;
- **Step Four:** The Learning Engine analyzes consumer responses and automatically adjusts consumer preferences in the model (expressed as probabilities) to better reflect consumer preferences. New content is sent to consumers based on the new digital profile;
- **Step Five:** The Learning Engine transmits updated information to a Personal Memory database where consumers' media profiles are created and constantly updated.

Steps Four and Five continue indefinitely: Based on its algorithmic learning process, the AI engine continually refines consumers' media profiles and accurately predicts consumer content and product interests and choices in varying contexts.

3. Establishing the DNA of Journalistic Content

Since the early 1990s, major interdisciplinary research efforts have been invested in developing efficient ways to automatically retrieve information and knowledge from multimedia journalistic content, primarily to enable consumers to find information they seek quickly and accurately. The community of researchers involved in what became known as multimedia information retrieval research (MIRA) covers many fields, including natural language processing (NLP), human computer interaction (HCI), information theory (IT), statistics, and pattern recognition, to name a few. MIRA is based on emerging interdisciplinary multimedia research and systems dealing with conventional and big multimedia data, and specifically focuses on "new applications and services that can analyze, retrieve, classify, and annotate multimedia information even for big multimedia data, as well as to help establish semantical and contextual connections among users on the basis of the information of their interest" (http://www.sitis-conf.org/en/multimedia-information-retrieval-and-applications-mira.php).

Most research tools divide content into small digital content units, analyze and tag these sub-units, and finally perform an integrative analysis to conceptualize the entire content in a way that is meaningful for consumers. In some applications, visual content is converted into mathematical formulations that can then be subjected to analysis based on AI algorithms [Jeon *et al.*, 2003].

These efforts can be traced to mid-nineteenth-century French author George Polti (b. 1868), who analyzed the elements of successful literature. Based on an analysis of classical Greek texts and French literature, Polti compiled a list of 36 dramatic situations that featured in good dramas, such as prayer to the supernatural, crime pursued by vengeance, loss or recovery of a lost one, disaster, remorse, revolt against a tyrant, and enigma. Polti's list remains popular and writers often use it in developing stories; even *Shrek* scriptwriter Terry Rusio admitted to having referred to Polti's list to resolve a situation in the film's plot. Polti's analysis of the DNA of drama was followed by other writers who also attempted to discover good story elements and persuasive drama, not written from an information-retrieval perspective, but provide the literary "blobs" that allow researchers to dissect a story along its content elements.

4. Content-Based Image and Video Retrieval (CBIVR)

The primary strategy used to enable image retrieval or automatic conceptualization of visual content is to divide visual frames into smaller sections or areas called "blobs" using statistical methods such as clustering. Each blob is annotated with a descriptive text that employs categories such as color, texture, shape, and structure. Statistical theories are then used to associate words with image regions that are then compared with human manual annotations of similar images [Smeulders *et al.*, 2000]. Gradually, a "vocabulary of blobs" is built up and used to describe images [Duygulu *et al.*, 2002].

To develop automatic retrieval methods that do not rely on subjective human analysis, images are segmented by features such as color, texture differences, shapes, and other salient points, which requires techniques that identify thresholds between color histograms corresponding to consecutive video frames [Flickner *et al.*, 1995]. CBIVR researchers develop mathematical descriptions of the images, or "signatures", which allow computers to measure content similarities between image frames based on statistical methods such as clustering and classification. Search engines such as ImageSpace allow users to directly query multiple visual objects, such as sky, trees, and water, and are essentially the same tools used by law enforcement officers in performing automatic detection of pornographic content [Flickner *et al.*, 1995].

A major effort in automatic tagging (or captioning) of video content was initiated by Facebook, which understands the importance of automatic dissemination of content based on consumers' digital profiles.

"Facebook is making big strides in using its artificial intelligence systems for image recognition, but it's also working on bringing this technology to video. … it has a team working on automatically tagging people in videos. … the idea here is to allow you to search for people in any of the videos they have shared with you … Facebook may be indexing this moment automatically for you … Facebook is also working on automatically captioning videos, and it is conceivable that it could use the same image-recognition techniques for video that it uses for detecting objects in still images" [Lardinois, 2016].

Another major player in automatic video tagging is IBM, whose Watson program develops algorithms for an automatic visual recognition system based on advanced machine learning of images that can be trained by users to improve recognition accuracy over time (https://www.ibm.com/watson/services/visual-recognition/).

5. Human-Centered Content Search

It has long been recognized that human satisfaction with search for knowledge and information in multimedia content involves several dimensions, including a mixture of rational and emotional dimensions. To capture these dimensions in order to reduce errors and increase user satisfaction, content-based image retrieval (CBIR) researchers realize that integrating human feedback and involvement in automatic multi-model content analysis is crucial. This understanding led to efforts in what became known as "human-centered computing".

Moreover, each consumer's search is specific to the context of the search and the emotional state of the consumer. Consequently, identical search results may be judged differently at different times, even by the same person, based on his or her emotional state at the time of the search. The understanding that satisfaction with search results is a function of a person's background, education, and values, as well as his or her emotional state, prompted the development of the field of affective computing [Barnard *et al.*, 2003], which is the study and measurement of the emotions or what Datta *et al.* [2006] refer to as the "aesthetic dimension" that a certain piece of content evokes in people. Work by Salway and Graham [2003] illustrates efforts to define images according to emotional categories. These researchers developed a way to extract character emotions from films based on a model that links character emotions to events in their environment.

6. Media Engagement

In the pre-Internet period, the economic engine driving journalism in the non-public service media was advertising-based. Journalism companies, regardless of the media platform (paper, video, or audio), sold consumer attention to advertisers, which was mainly measured by ratings, which were recognized to be inaccurate. Today, the interactive nature of the new media platforms allows for a more scientific and individualized measurement of consumer attention along personal dimensions, creating a competition for consumer attention that is more fierce and complex than ever. The media industry is constantly developing new ways to measure consumer attention across multiple parameters, including consumers' cognitive and behavioral profiles and the contextual factors of consumption.

In this new battle for consumer attention, the concept of engagement is used to describe the relations between consumers and the journalistic content. According to the definition developed by The Advertising Research Council (ARC), media engagement is "turning on a prospect to a brand idea enhanced by the surrounding context …". This working definition captures marketers' ultimate objective of linking brand advertising with positive affect toward a brand, within the unique setting of program content [Kilger and Romer, 2007]. This focus on consumer engagement is based on the fundamental premise that more engaged consumers will spend more on the advertised product. Kilger and Romer studied the effect of media engagement and product-purchase probabilities across three media platforms — television, Internet, and printed magazines, and consistently found that as engagement measures increased so did the mean likelihood of products advertised in the media to be purchased.

Kilger and Romer [2007] argue that consumer engagement in a journalistic content can be enhanced through three mechanisms: cognitive (triggered by the relevance of the program and advertisement to the consumer), emotional (triggered by the consumer's positive regard for the content and advertising), and behavioral (the consumer's attention to the program and advertising content). This recognition by the advertising world, that engagement in journalistic content involves consumer cognition, emotional profile, and behavior is relevant for efforts to perfect computer-based information retrieval as applied to content and context analysis.

7. Behavioral and Contextual Targeting of Journalistic Content

For the advertising industry, the ultimate goal of tracking and measuring engagement is to enhance behavioral targeting: directing advertisements to consumers based on contextual and personal parameters identified by Kilger and Romer [2007]: cognitions, emotions, and behavior. Most Internet giants, including Google, Microsoft, and Yahoo, are involved in behavioral targeting. Google confirms this in its official website. Google's first generation of behavioral targeting used two separate systems, Adwords and AdSense. Adwords targets ads based on the search subject matter by identifying search keywords, while AdSense targets ads based on website content the consumer views. "For example if you visit a gardening site, ads on that site may be related to gardening" [Kassner, 2009].

The major players in this field have transitioned from early uses of behavioral targeting based on text analysis and are now developing automatic image and video tagging, which will generate huge quantities of data of potential value for product targeting. AdSense, for example, was extended to search annotated images and videos in YouTube. Once image and video content are analyzed and annotated automatically, behavioral targeting will likely be applied to all journalistic content.

The industry is now moving toward an integration of behavioral and contextual targeting. According to Jacobs [2016], "Contextual targeting is ad placement done smartly. Rather than relying on broad demographics, location, and simple browsing history, contextually-targeted ads connect the right message to the right person at the right time ... Behavioral targeting is done in a similar fashion in that it uses cookies to determine the best ads to deliver to the prospect based on their browsing history" (http://www.databilities.net/2016/09/20/contextual-targeting-vs-behavioral-targeting/). Contextual targeting is considered more effective than behavioral targeting especially if it addresses the three engagement categories: cognitions, emotions, and behavior. AI algorithms promise to facilitate the integration of behavioral and contextual targeting for optimal targeting.

Behavioral targeting raises serious privacy issues, which have been discussed extensively in academic literature and political circles. Tim Berners-Lee, credited with inventing the World Wide Web, addressed the UK parliament on privacy and the Internet, and stated that he came to "raise awareness to the technical, legal and ethical implications of the interception and profiling by ISPs in collaboration with behavioral targeting companies" [Watson, 2009]. The issue of privacy warrants a comprehensive discussion, which unfortunately is beyond the scope of this chapter.

8. Behavioral Targeting in Social Networks

Social networks characterized by voluntary profiling by members who upload personal data in texts, images, and videos provide fertile ground for behavioral targeting, which has become the basis of the business models of all leading Internet giants. As behavioral targeting comes to include journalistic content, human journalists will be judged by their media organizations according to their ROI, which is, in turn, a direct function of the number of their social network followers.

All major social networks including Facebook, Instagram, Twitter, and Pinterest allow their consumers to browse and purchase products within their social network platforms, which are becoming the new marketplace for all products, including journalistic products and news stories. In 2016, Snapchat's director of revenue operations Clement Xue announced that it would introduce behavioral targeting for advertisers in 2016 [O'Reilly, 2016].

"With around 93 percent of Millennials spending regular time on social networks, ecommerce is now spreading directly onto social media channels. As mobile browsing and purchasing becomes more normalized, it's likely that this trend will continue to grow in 2017 .... Users trust their social media networks, and increasingly they are coming to these networks on the hunt for new, interesting content ..." [Foster, 2017].

9. Managing Digital Identities — Developing a Universal Standard

A consumer's digital identity is a vital component in the behavioral targeting process and directly affects the type of services and information a consumer receives. The global knowledge industry invests great resources in developing and improving methods of digital identity management. One such example is called "federated identity management", which represents a global standard for consumer identification on multiple trusted platforms, to enhance users' convenience and efficiency [Gartner, 2017]. According to this standard, various components of users' profiles are collected while they surf on different sites and social networks, and consolidated into profiles that meet a form defined in a single global standard. The standard has been successfully adopted by financial organizations, academic institutions, the American electronic government initiative, and other organizations.

Significantly, the adoption of international standards for defining digital identities will allow marketers to track surfers in any site in cyberspace and conduct widespread studies on the connection between the users' digital identities, personalities, fields of interest, and cognitive abilities. Data-mining "robots", which are IA algorithms, automatically analyze texts, video, and audio contents and transform them into personal digital identity (or sociological DNA) [Lemelshtrich Latar, 2004] for any person, based on analyses of all the actions that he or she performs on the Internet. Furthermore, AI algorithms can be applied to automatically identify surfers' uniquely dynamic ways of surfing, which are a function of a person's memory, ability to make decisions, and additional cognitive factors, in a never-ending process that is continually revised as long as the person is active on the Internet.

10. Socio-Genetics, Digital Identities, and the Future of Journalism

Science is constantly improving our knowledge about the connections between mind and body. For example, we know today that social behavior is linked to genetics. Understanding these connections and how they work in social contexts is valuable for analyzing the body, mind, and ecosystem surrounding them and therefore such understanding makes a powerful contribution to the construction of digital identities. In fact, in the construction of digital identities, information about a person's genetic codes may be as important as the information from his or her social networks.

Since the completion of the Human Genome Project in 2001, commercial competition has arisen between companies to produce machines that map the genetic code of man, and research and instrumentation for gene sequencing, or mapping a person's genetic code, are developing rapidly at leading research institutes and major commercial companies worldwide. Illumina, a leader in developing gene sequencing devices, declared that its cost per individual gene sequencing may soon be less than USD 100 [Keshavan, 2017].

The entry of information-age giants such as Google and leading research centers such as Harvard and Cornell into the field of genetic research, will close the knowledge research gaps much faster. The large volume of participants in these studies, the vast databases holding participants' digital identities, data mining efforts to document peoples' online social interactions, together with the use of smart algorithms, is helping science to begin to predict social behavior — both pro-social and anti-social — based on genetic mapping.

From the point of view of the practice of journalism, the emergence of digital identities suggests that publishers and journalists will be able to simulate and measure how their news stories and storytelling will impact audiences and other stakeholders, even as they are developing their stories. Digital identities thus will introduce interesting opportunities and challenges for human journalists. For example, consider a situation where readers use their digital identities, combined with a series of filters, to select news stories they want to be brought to their attention. Let's say the quality of the filters and digital identities is good enough to estimate both the chance that a story will catch the readers' attention and the chance it will lead to action by the readers. Now consider a set of contextual advertisers who will pay for readers' attention and the opportunity to interact with them. Consider a journalist who, when writing a story, has access both to readers' digital identities and filters, and access to the contextual advertisers. The journalist can test the story on digital identities that represent interested readers and advertisers interested in these readers, as the story is written, adjusting the writing to obtain the optimal results in terms of the aims of the journalist, the audience, and the advertisers. In this case, the journalist would, for all practical purposes, be manipulating the news: producing a story would be equated to solving a dynamic equation involving the journalist, the audience, and the business models of media organizations, which might lead to the death of journalistic freedom.

References

Barnard, K., Duygulu, P., Forsyth, D., de Freitas, N., Nlei, D. M., and Jordan, M. I. (2003). Matching words and pictures. *Journal of Machine Learning Research*, 3, 1107–1135.

Datta, R., Joshi, D., Li, J., and Wang, J. Z. (2006). Studying aesthetics in photographic images using computational approach. In *Proceedings of Computer Vision — ECCV 2006, 9th European Conference on Computer Vision*. Gratz, Austria May 7. doi: 10.1007/11744078_23.

Doctor, K. (2013). The newsonomics of 'Little Data,' data scientists and conversion specialists. *NiemanLab*. Retrieved from http://www.niemanlab.org/2013/10/the-newsonomics-of-little-data-data-scientists-and-conversion-specialists/

Duygulu, P., Barnard, K., de Freitas, N., and Forsyth, D. (2002). Object recognition as machine translation: Learning a lexicon for fixed image vocabulary. In *Proceedings of the Seventh European Conference on Computer Vision* (pp. 97–112). London: Springer-Verlag.

Flickner, M., Sawhney, H., Niblack, W., *et al.* (1995). Query by image and video content: The QBIC system. *Computer,* 28(9), 23–32.

Foster, P. (2017). Ecommerce social marketing media marketing trends to focus on in 2017. *JustUno.* Retrieved from blog.justuno.com/ecommerce-social-media-marketing-trends-2017

Gartner. (2017). *Federated Identity Management.* Gartner IT Glossary. Retrieved from http://www.gartner.com/it-glossary/federated-identity-management

Jacobs, O. (2016). Contextual targeting vs. behavioral targeting. *Databili-ties,* Retrieved from http://www.databilities.net/2016/09/20/contextual-targeting-vs-behavioral-targeting/

Jeon, J., Lavrenko, V., and Manmatha, R. (2003). Automatic image annotation and retrieval using cross media relevance models. In *Proceedings of the 26th Annual International ACM SIGIR Conference on Research and Development in Information Retrieval* (pp. 119–126). http://doi.acm.org/10.1145/860435.860459

Kassner, M. (2009). Google quietly starts behavioral targeting. *ZDNetAsia.*

Keshavan, M. (2017). Illumina says it can deliver a USD 100 genome soon. StatPlus.

Kilger, M. and Romer, E. (2007). Do measures of media engagement correlate with product purchase likelihood? *Journal of Advertising Research,* 47(3), 313–325.

Lardinois, F. (2016). Facebook will soon be able to automatically tag your friends in videos. *TechCrunch.*

Lemelshtrich Latar, N. (2004). *Personal web social DNA and cybernetic decision making,* Paper presented at the annual meeting of the International Communication Association, New Orleans Sheraton, New Orleans. Retrieved from http://www.allacademic.com/meta/p112756_index.html

Lemelshtrich Latar, N. and Nordfors, D. (2009). Digital identities and journalism content. *Innovation Journalism,* 6(7), 4–47.

O'Reilly, L. (2016). Snapchat is about to introduce something advertisers have been waiting for ages: Behavioral targeting. *Business Insider.* Retrieved from http://www.businessinsider.com/snapchat-to-launch-behavioral-targeting-for-adver tisers-2016-8

Salway, A. and Graham, M. (2003). Extracting information about emotions in films. In *Proceedings of the Eleventh ACM International Conference on Multimedia,* November 2–8, pp. 299–302.

Smeulders, A. W. M., Worring, M., Santini, S., Gupta, A., and Jain, R. (2000). Content based image retrieval at the end of the early years. *IEEE Transactions on Pattern Analysis and Machine Intelligence,* 22(12), 1349–1380.

Watson, F. (2009). Behavioral targeting: Profiling or projecting user experience. *Search Engine Watch.*

Williamson, D. A. (2005). White Paper on behavioral targeting. *Wall Street Journal* and *eMarketer.*

Section Two:

New Story Telling in the Age of AI

Chapter 6

"The new news": Storytelling in the digital age

Gali Einav and Nathan Lipson

"I know only one thing about the technologies that await us in the future: we will find ways to tell stories with them" — Jason Ohler, author of *Digital and Traditional Storytelling* and *Four Big Ideas for the Future*.

The media industry has been undergoing accelerated change, driven largely by the proliferation of digital platforms. This transformation is sometimes referred to as the "Third Technological Revolution", following the printing press and the industrial revolutions. Its enormous impact transcends technology and engenders substantial changes across society [Einav, 2014], as new digital media platforms, including Smartphones and social networks, fundamentally affect the way we communicate with one another. In this chapter, we argue that the adoption of digital technologies and the resulting media habits have not only transformed interpersonal communication norms, but have also transformed storytelling as we know it. We refer to the new approaches to storytelling adopted by brands, advertisers, news platforms, and journalists, as the "New News Story". We begin this chapter by exploring the key consumer behavior trends related to the sweeping adoption of digital media platforms and their impact on how brands communicate with their consumers. The second part of the chapter focuses on how adoption of digital media platforms has transformed storytelling in the news industry.

1. Key Consumer Behavior Trends

The most significant changes in media use patterns are clustered in the age groups referred to by marketers and researchers as "Generation Y", born between 1977 and 1992, and younger generations, referred to as "Generation Z" or "digital natives" [Zickuhr, 2010]. Daily time spent on digital platforms more than doubled between 2014 and 2016, reaching more than four hours a day, driven mostly by mobile phone use, which is dominated by these groups: Younger users (18–24 year olds) spend roughly half of their time (49%) per day on mobile devices compared to 13% of the day among 65+ year olds. Young people spend half as much time watching television as older viewers over age 65 (21 versus 46 hours per week, respectively), yet twice as much time online and mobile video viewing [Nielsen, 2015].

Since 2005, social networking use has leaped from 10% to 76% of Internet users, with close to 90% penetration among users between the ages of 18 and 29, although use by older age groups has also grown [Perrin, 2015]. The substantial increase in time spent on social media has been attributed mainly to the increasing accessibility afforded by mobile devices. Across social media, online video usage, which includes messaging platforms such as Instagram, Facebook, WhatsApp, and FB messenger, has also skyrocketed, fueled mainly by the increasing popularity of posting and sharing of user-generated video, and photo sharing, reaching more than 3 billion photos shared per day over various messaging platforms [Meeker, 2017].

Additional technologies and platforms are seeing increased use, again mostly by younger generations. The Virtual Reality (VR) market, for example, is predicted to reach $38 billion by 2020, 20 times its value in 2016 [Super Data, 2017]. Although the relatively high cost of dedicated virtual reality hardware is a deterrent to widespread adoption, consumers are showing considerable interest in using VR for travel, entertainment, events, home design, and education [Greenlight Insights, 2016]. Another technology trend with broad implications is voice-activated AI platforms such as WhatsApp Voice, Google Voice, Amazon Echo, and Apple's Siri. The increased ease and convenience of voice-based social search represents a new form of communication that is improving in accuracy and predicted to grow [Meeker, 2017]. Gamification is becoming more of a mainstream practice as gamified content has become recognized as a driver of consumer engagement and loyalty across digital platforms [Mak, 2016]. As a result, the gamification market is estimated to have increased tenfold since 2015.

While Facebook remains the largest global social network, with almost 2 billion monthly active users [Zephoria Digital Marketing, 2017], younger users have shifted to other platforms such as Instagram (which was acquired by Facebook in April 2012) and Twitter, and messaging platforms such as WhatsApp (acquired by Facebook in October 2014) and Snapchat, which is discussed further later. As Facebook became the "platform for everyone", including parents, grandparents, and bosses, the ubiquity of the platform gradually reduced its appeal for younger users.

Other main drivers of this shift include a desire, particularly among younger consumers, for greater control, privacy, and instantaneousness of their communications. For example, new definitions of privacy emphasize controlling who will see the message, rather than the content of the message itself [Boyd, 2014], a task that becomes increasingly complex in view of Facebook's continually evolving algorithms that determine content exposure. Sensitive to users' desire to control multiple aspects of their content, mobile-based messaging platforms such as Instagram, WhatsApp, and Snapchat have built sizable networks by empowering users to control their audience and effectively control distribution. Snapchat, the ephemeral social network on which short video messages or "Snaps" disappear after they are viewed by recipients, offers a new level of control, immediacy, and privacy. Consumer appreciation of these features spurred Snapchats' rapid adoption, and daily active users now surpass 150 million [Smith, 2017], with the majority of users under age 25.

Driven by Snapchat, the emphasis on protecting privacy norms is now reproduced in competing platforms that cater to older demographics. For example, Facebook has incorporated a Stories feature into Instagram, WhatsApp, and Facebook Messenger, and now, Instagram's private messages also vanish after 24 hours. Facebook also incorporated features similar to Snapchat Lenses, which offers an additional avenue for self-expression through photos [Heath, 2016].

Storytelling formats, including many that evolved over the last 100 years, are also in transition [Weiler, 2015], as messaging and texts have fundamentally affected our approach toward self-expression. For example, attention spans of young people are 60% shorter than those of the previous generation. Digital natives increasingly focus on new forms of self-expression built around consumer media and use trends that are mostly visual, brief, and often short lived, such as Twitter (originally limited to 140 characters and recently increased to 280), and employ a short-form communication messaging style used on platforms such as WhatsApp or WeChat. Equally transformative has been the role of emoticons as replacements for word descriptions of emotions, and the more general use of visual representations to replace text [Meeker, 2017] that younger generations may regard as "TLDR" ("too long, didn't read").

Although older generations might tend to judge these formats critically, these changes are not necessarily a negative trend for social communication. The new communication language used by digital-savvy audiences brings with it new meanings and contexts. Harper [2010] argues that texting represents an authentic expression of the true self, rather than a manifestation of narcissistic "Me Generation" behaviors. Katz and Crocker [2015] found that Snapchat selfies and selfie-related practices enabled meaningful "language games" that use images as both grammar and vocabulary, and as such, "constitute a major step forward in visual communication within contemporary culture" (para. 5).

Communication trends associated with the younger demographics are gradually being adopted by older audiences. Since the media consumption habits of younger generations generally gain mainstream acceptance, it is not surprising that the "New Normal" is a world in which people are constantly connected through devices and social networks and in which the expectation of choice, control, and personalization are a given. There is, however, little stability in this new norm, as "technological generations" may be overtaken within as few as five years due to the accelerated pace of technology adoption.

2. Reinventing Storytelling: Brands Rise to the Challenge of the "Snapchat Generation"

Snapchat is an excellent example of a platform that incorporates many of the emerging consumer behavior trends, including direct messaging, brief visual communications, video and photo sharing, as well as a new sense of privacy; yet Snapchat's 10-second framework for telling a story requires a new form of narrative. Brands that seek to reach a young digital-savvy demographic and establish an emotional connection with them, must communicate with them in their own language [Marci, 2015]. As the adoption of such platforms expands, brands that are unable to tell their story in 10 seconds may lose relevance. Similar storytelling frameworks include Vine (which ceased operations in 2016), a platform on which users share 6-second messages via Twitter, which is used by brands to quickly disseminate messages. For example, during the 2016 Super Bowl, Tide supplemented its traditional commercials with 20 6-second Vine stories that conversed with the aired TV commercials (such as a Vine story on how to remove ketchup stains following a Heinz Ketchup commercial; Cream, 2014).

Another example of how brands are communicating in the new digital language is YouTube's 6-second un-skippable mobile video "bumper ads" that were introduced in 2016 and defined as "Little Haikus of Video" [Johnson, 2016]. Like the short-form story format introduced by Snapchat, this format takes into account that content is accessed on mobile devices, which are characterized by shorter attention spans.

A more direct use of the new forms of storytelling can be traced to the 2013 introduction of "Snapchat Stories". Each story comprised a series of images or short video "snaps" of up to 1 minute long that disappear within 24 hours. The launch of "Our Stories", which offered brands and publishers a platform to reach a large audience of younger users, primarily under age 25, expanded storytelling from individual accounts to publishers. "Discover", introduced by Snapchat in 2015, created branded channels to help users find publisher stories. In 2016, Discover was later relaunched to provide a sense of curated content by adding short titles to each story to gauge user interest in the content.

Building on the rising trend of gamification as a form of engagement, Playbuzz (www.playbuzz.com) created an authoring and distribution platform for interactive storytelling. Playbuzz allows individual users as well as publishers and advertisers to utilize its platform to create various forms of games around content, enabling an entire environment that might better attract millennials and younger generations. As described by Shaul Olmert, Playbuzz co-founder and CEO: "The publishing industry must adapt to the new reality of online consumption habits … content creators can no longer approach penning content in an outdated manner, and must start to rely on tools that will enable them to tell impactful stories that are stimulating both visually and from a narrative perspective" [MMG, 2017].

Playbuzz storytelling techniques emphasize visual over text to "gamify storytelling", which is manifested mostly in the form of short quizzes. For example, Playbuzz created a Ford campaign quiz that prompted users to choose what color car they would prefer. The game format engages users and provides valuable insights on consumer preferences that would be difficult to obtain through a traditional ad format.

Playbuzz reports an 85–95% item completion rate, a 5–10% share rate, and 2–4 minutes attention per session. The platform has built up a substantial network of more than 500 million monthly active users who interact with its content in 40 different languages, potentially impacting the future of storytelling for publishers and brands. The new shorter, personalized, gamified, and visual forms of storytelling used by brands have also filtered down into the way storytelling is used to tell the news, which is elaborated in the following section.

3. "The New News"

"We have not yet created a news report that takes full advantage of all the storytelling tools at our disposal and, in the process, does the best possible job of speaking to our potential audience." —*The New York Times* 2020 Group Report, January 2017.

As far as the press is concerned, the Internet has proven itself to be the most powerful force to influence the news industry in the last 100 years. Much more than radio, TV, and cable TV, the Internet has overturned many of the basic tenets of the news industry since its inception and has driven many news organizations to extinction and others to an uncertain future. *The New York Times* is an example of a newspaper that has made significant strides into the digital age. It uses an increasing variety of interactive tools to tell stories, and set a goal not shared by many others: focusing on paid digital subscriptions as a source of revenue growth instead of ad revenues. This decision, as well as the precipitous decline of ad revenues, resulted in a situation where revenues driven by readers surpassed ad revenues. Additionally, in the first quarter of 2017, *The New York Times* added 308,000 digital-only news subscribers ("the Trump Bump"), the biggest quarterly addition in the newspaper's history, reaching a total of 2.2 million digital subscribers. According to the 2020 Report, in 2016, "the Times brought in almost $500 million in purely digital revenue, which is far more than the digital revenues reported by many other leading publications (including BuzzFeed, *The Guardian*, and *The Washington Post*) — combined" [Leonhardt *et al.*, 2017].

But as inspiring as it is, *The New York Times'* story is irrelevant to most newspapers — not only in the US, but across the world. *The New York Times* has an unparalleled reputation, a — still — huge newsroom and an outstanding concentration of editorial and business talent. It is also profitable, with more than USD 800 million in cash. Other newspapers, even those with high credibility and a relatively large readership, are in a much more precarious position, with smaller newsrooms, less financial resources, less prestige, smaller markets, more competition from other newspapers, and especially from Google and Facebook. Many are not too far from going out of business — or being saved by deep-pocketed oligarchs who may have less-than-pure journalistic agendas.

Thus, although the Internet has unleashed a huge wave of innovation, almost all of it occurred outside of the traditional journalist landscape. Several new news players have become so successful that they have been able to capture considerable consumer attention and businesses' ad dollars. Two of them — Facebook and Google — are now responsible for around 70% of news organizations' traffic [Parse.ly, n.d.].

These new players are using innovative methods for telling stories and engaging readers in ways that were not previously available, specifically through mobile device apps, VR, and chatbots. Compared with other Internet tools, these new forms of storytelling are widely used by young readers — the demographic that consumes less and less news and can help guarantee a better future for the news industry.

Although not all new hugely-successful digital apps and services can be of value for news organizations, the many that are of value involve diverse storytelling formats such as text, images, and video, or any combination of these three. Not only do they offer new technology, they also offer extremely large distribution networks or communities of followers. In addition to the new storytelling tools described below, many more tools such as Google AMP (www.ampproject.org), Instagram, podcasts, and Slack (www.slack.com) are in use.

4. Snapchat Stories

As previously mentioned, Snapchat, launched in 2011, was originally a tool for sharing self-destructing images with friends. This feature alone was enough to make it extremely popular, but in late 2013 a new feature was introduced: Snapchat Stories. Contrary to the original feature, images shared on users' Stories feed can be viewed by all the poster's Snapchat friends and are accessible for 24 hours, after which they disappear.

Snapchat Stories retained the ephemerality of the original snaps, which stresses freshness, but added the ability to *tell a story* with a collection of images and videos from the past 24 hours. The stories are very easy to consume, which fits the ever-diminishing attention span of consumers. In January 2015, with the introduction of Discover [Crook, 2015], the needs of publishers were specifically addressed. The business relationship started off with a revenue-sharing model in which publishers keep 70% of ads they sell and 50% of ads sold by Snapchat [McDermott, 2015], but then changed to a model whereby Snapchat pays publishers a licensing fee and retains all ad revenues [Kafka, 2016]. As of June 2017, Discover featured Mashable, BuzzFeed, *Cosmopolitan*, CNN, *National Geographic*, and others. Clicking on a publisher's tile launches its recent stories.

At least some publishers that participate in the intentionally limited cadre of Snapchat Stories participants seem happy. In September 2015, BuzzFeed's Jonah Peretti stated that Snapchat was BuzzFeed's third biggest source of traffic [Kulwin, 2015].

5. Facebook Instant Articles

In May 2015, Facebook launched Instant Articles [Constine, 2015], which allows publishers to display entire articles inside Facebook's mobile apps, retaining the original look and feel of the articles at the publishers' discretion. Instant Articles supports the use of all popular measuring and tracking services to ensure traffic is not "lost". Publishers also retain all the revenues from ads sold within Instant Articles (if ads are sold by Facebook, publishers retain 70% of the revenues). However, when Facebook subsequently limited how and where publishers could place ads and changed its News Feed algorithm to place less weight on their content [Backstrom, 2016], more and more publishers opted out of the service [Moses, 2017].

6. Chatbots

Bots are designed to automate tasks. Chatbots, a sub-group of bots, are input–output software units that simulate conversations and are usually hosted on messaging apps such as Twitter and Facebook. In fact, Twitter hosts some of the best-known bots, including a bot that auto-tweets whenever a 5-plus earthquake is registered with the USGS (https://twitter.com/earthquakeBot). Chatbots can be complex, but since they are hosted on communication apps, where user attention span is short, they tend to be very simple. Because they are relatively simple to build, several news-related chatbots, such as *The Washington Post*'s "Feels Bot", are developed *ad hoc*. Feels Bot, which was hosted on Facebook [*The Washington Post*, n.d.], was launched one month before the US presidential elections, and posed the following single question: How do you feel about the election? To respond, users selected one of the five emojis. Using this chatbot, *The Washington Post*'s readers had an opportunity to express their emotions and track the emotions of others on the bot's dedicated accessible database.

7. 360° Virtual Reality Videos

360° videos allow viewers to experience their surroundings as if they were in the filmed location, with views changing as viewers look in different directions. Virtual reality, which is sometimes considered synonymous with 360° videos, offers extremely immersive experiences. VR and 360° videos can be used to experience real-world scenes, help recreate historic situations, and walk viewers through imaginary, perhaps futuristic, scenes. Use normally entails special hardware, such as a headset, and outputs may include human-made elements.

One example of a 360° video produced by a news organization is *The Guardian*'s "6 × 9: Solitary Confinement" (6 × 9: A virtual experience of solitary confinement, 2016) In this video, which requires viewing hardware, the viewer enters "a US solitary confinement prison cell and tells the story of the psychological damage that can ensue from isolation". *The New York Times* developed a standalone app for its own VR work, nytvr (http://www.nytimes.com/marketing/nytvr), which currently contains dozens of videos that are available for viewing, with or without a headset. While VR/360° videos offer the most compelling way of storytelling by immersing consumers into the reported event, costs are still extremely high (approximately USD 10,000 per minute produced) and the best results require hardware, which also represents significant costs for consumers [Giardina, 2016].

8. Monetization

None of the new storytelling tools, including those mentioned above as well as Google AMP, Instagram, Podcasts, Slack, and many others, have developed into profitable operations. Indeed, some may still be in the experimental phase, which almost invariably implies an absence of revenues altogether. Many more new tools fail to even complete the development process: In January, *New York Magazine's* CEO Pamela Wasserstein said that "… we just want to make sure that if we're putting something out there, it's providing something different and filling a need" [Owen, 2017].

In January 2017, Digital Content Next (formerly, Online Publishers Association), a US trade association of digital content companies, issued a report on revenues of publishers using third-party platforms such as Facebook and Snapchat [Digital Content Next, 2017]. The report found that monetization of third-party platforms in the first half of 2016 represented an estimated average revenue of USD 7.7 million per company for the 17 participating members providing revenue data (mainly major publications), or approximately 14% of their total revenues for the period; 85% of that revenue, about USD 6.5 million, came from video content, and primarily from ads.

While these tools are attractive, it is still impossible to determine whether they can attract enough young readers and generate enough income to support the news industry over the longer term. It is equally difficult to predict if they will not quickly become obsolete and be replaced by newer technologies and applications that also require experimentation and development. While *The New York Times*, arguably the leader in innovation and experimentation among traditional newspapers, has the resources to invest in experimentation and development, the vast majority of newspapers have very limited resources available for innovation development, and therefore much narrower error margins.

Finally, it is important to note that the innovation process in itself plays an important role in the development of the newsroom culture and its adoption of an innovative mindset. While a newspaper may have no choice (due to paucity of resources) but to sit on the sidelines and attentively observe how leading newspapers explore such new experimentations, they are undoubtedly missing an important learning opportunity. Experience in innovation not only enhances a newsroom's innovative mindset and culture, it also may be the only chance for survival in today's world of rapidly changing technology.

References

Backstrom, L. (2016). News feed FYI: Helping make sure you don't miss stories from friends. *Facebook Newsroom.* Retrieved from https://newsroom.fb.com/news/2016/06/news-feed-fyi-helping-make-sure-you-dont-miss-stories-from-friends/

Boyd, D. (2014). *It's Complicated — The Social Lives of Networked Teens.* New Haven, CT: Yale University Press.

Constine, J. (2015). Facebook starts hosting publishers' "instant articles". *TechCrunch.* Retrieved from https://techcrunch.com/2015/05/12/facebook-instant-articles/

Cream (2014). Tide Super Bowl Vine. *Cream.* Retrieved from http://www.creamglobal.com/case-studies/latest/17798/36267/tide-super-bowl-vine/

Crook, J. (2015). Snapchat launches Discover. *TechCrunch*. Retrieved from https://techcrunch.com/2015/01/27/snapchat-launches-discover/

Digital Content Next. (2017). *Distributed Content Revenue Benchmark Report — New*. Retrieved from www.amic.media/media/files/file_352_1134.pdf

Einav, G. (Ed.). (2014). Back to the future: Consumer and business trends in the digital age. In G. Einave (Ed.), *The New World of Transitioned Media — Digital Realignment and Industry Transformation* (pp. 1–7). New York: Springer.

Giardina, C. (2016). Cine Gear: Virtual reality stitching can cost $10,000 per finished minute. *The Hollywood Reporter*. Retrieved from http://www.hollywoodreporter.com/node/899697

Greenlight Insights. (2016). *2016 Virtual Reality Consumer Adoption Report*. Retrieved from https://greenlightinsights.com/industry-analysis/consumer-vr-reports-2016/

Harper, R. (2010). *Texture: Human Expression in the Age of Communication Overload*. Cambridge. MA: MIT Press.

Heath, A. (2016). Facebook is copying Snapchat's geofilters by letting people make their own camera "frames". *Business Insider*. Retrieved from http://www.businessinsider.com/facebook-copies-snapchat-geofilters-with-camera-frames-2016-12

Johnson, L. (2016). YouTube builds "little haikus of video" with no 6-second mobile ads. *Adweek*. Retrieved from http://www.adweek.com/digital/youtube-builds-little-haikus-video-new-6-second-mobile-ads-171052/

Kafka, P. (2016). Snapchat wants to stop sharing ad revenue with its media partners. *Recode*. Retrieved from https://www.recode.net/2016/10/18/13326196/snapchat-discover-ad-sales-plan-change

Katz, J. E. and Crocker, A. T. (2015). Selfies and photo messaging as visual conversation: Reports from the United States, United Kingdom and China. *International Journal of Communication, 9*, 1861–1872.

Kulwin, N. (2015). This week on "Re/code Decode": CEO Jonah Peretti explains how BuzzFeed won the Internet (Updated). *Recode*. Retrieved from https://www.recode.net/2015/9/16/11618618/this-week-on-recode-decode-ceo-jonah-peretti-explains-how-buzzfeed

Leonhardt, D., Rudoren, J., Galinsky, J., Skog, K., Lavey, M., Giratikanon, T., and Evans, T. (2017). The New York Times' 2020 Group Report. *The New York Times*. Retrieved from https://www.nytimes.com/projects/2020-report

Mak, H. W. (2016). 5 examples gamification in consumer engagement space. *Gamification*. Retrieved from http://www.gamification.co/2016/03/10/5-examples-gamification-consumer-engagement-space/

Marci, C. (2015). Storytelling in the digital media age. *TechCrunch*. Retrieved from www.techcrunch.com/2015/03/02/storytelling-in-the-digital-media-age/

McDermott, J. (2015). 5 (more) things we learned about Snapchat Discover. *Digiday*. Retrieved from https://digiday.com/media/5-things-learned-snapchat-dis cover/

Meeker, M. (2017). *Internet Trends 2017 — Code Conference*. Retrieved from Kleiner Perkins Website www.kpcb.com/Internet-trends

MMG Global Contributor. (2017). The NYT admits print is dead but we can still make people read again [blogpost]. *MMG*. Retrieved from http://mandmglobal.com/the-nyt-admits-print-is-dead-but-we-can-still-make-people-read-again/

Moses, L. (2017). Facebook faces increased publisher resistance to Instant Articles. *Digiday*. Retrieved from https://digiday.com/media/facebook-faces-increased-publisher-resistance-instant-articles/

Nielsen. (2015). Nielsen cross platform report Q1. Retrieved from: http://www.nielsen.com/us/en/insights/reports/2015/the-total-audience-report-q1-2015.html

Owen, L. H. (2017). Under its new CEO, New York Magazine is branching out into more "voice-y news products." *NiemanLab*. Retrieved from http://www.niemanlab.org/2017/01/under-its-new-ceo-new-york-magazine-is-branching-out-into-more-voice-y-news-products/

Parse.ly. (n.d.). *External Referral Traffic to Parse.ly Customers*. Retrieved from https://www.parse.ly/resources/data-studies/referrer-dashboard/

Perrin, A. (2015). Social media usage: 2005–2015. *Pew Research Center*. Retrieved from http://www.pewinternet.org/2015/10/08/social-networking-usage-2005-2015/

Smith, C. (2017). *135 Amazing Snapchat Statistics and Facts (June 2017)*. Retrieved from http://expandedramblings.com/index.php/snapchat-statistics/

Super Data. (2017). *Virtual Reality Market and Consumers*. Retrieved from https://www.super-dataresearch.com/market-data/virtual-reality-industry-report/

The Guardian. (2016). 6 × 9: A virtual experience of solitary confinement. *The Guardian*. Retrieved from https://www.theguardian.com/world/ng-interactive/2016/apr/27/6x9-a-virtual-experience-of-solitary-confinement

The Washington Post. (n.d.). *Feels*. Retrieved from https://www.washingtonpost.com/graphics/politics/facebook-messenger-elections-feels-bot/

Weiler, L. (2015). How storytelling has changed in the digital age. *World Economic Forum*. Retrieved from https://www.weforum.org/agenda/2015/01/how-storytelling-has-changed-in-the-digital-age/

Zephoria Digital Marketing. (2017). *The Top 20 Valuable Facebook Statistics — Updated July 2017*. Retrieved from https://zephoria.com/top-15-valuable-facebook-statistics

Zickuhr, K. (2010). *Generations 2010*. Pew Internet Research Internet & Technology Project. Retrieved from http://www.pewinternet.org/2010/12/16/generations-2010/

Chapter 7

Immersive journalism:
The new narrative

Doron Friedman and Candice Kotzen

Immersive journalism is a subcategory of journalism that uses virtual reality (VR) and similar technologies to provide those engaging in such technologies with a sense of being wholly engrossed in the news story, thus allowing the news audience to form a direct impression of the ambience of the story. This chapter is intended to serve as a primer of VR use for news storytelling for individuals with an interest or background in journalism. The first section presents some essential background on VR and related technologies. Next, we present some research findings on the impact of VR, and review some of the early work in immersive journalism. We conclude by delineating a collection of thoughts and questions for journalists wishing to enter into this new exciting field.

1. The Technology

More than 50 years after the first demonstration of virtual reality (VR) technologies [Sutherland, 1965], it is apparent that VR is on the brink of becoming a form of mass media as VR documentary and journalism has been a central theme. Triggered by Facebook's acquisition of Oculus Rift in 2014, the technology industry launched the race to deliver compelling VR hardware, software, and content. In this chapter, we present the essential background for non-experts who are intrigued by immersive journalism. For a recent comprehensive review of VR research in general, we recommend Slater and Sanchez-Vives [2016]. Relevant issues from this review are elaborated in this chapter.

VR aims at providing a total experience, by blocking information from the "real" world while providing high-fidelity multi-sensory information about an artificially generated reality. Current consumer VR systems only cater to the visual and auditory senses. One of the factors contributing to VR's high degree of illusion is sensorimotor contingencies that cause the content in the VR to change in response to the participant's head movements. In the real world, the images projected on our retina keep changing as our eyes continue to move several times per second, and our brain proactively generates the sensation of a stable external world. Unlike viewing a movie on an external display, immersion in VR is similar to real-world perception. This is one of the reasons that VR is perceived by the brain to be more "real" than movies. Other factors include stereoscopic depth information and the occlusion of external information.

The result is a subjective experience that is entirely different from any other mediated (or non-mediated) experience. Most individuals report that they feel as if they are transported to another place, rather than simply watching a movie. This phenomenon has been researched since the early 1990s, under the concept of presence in VR [Lombard and Ditton, 1997; Sanchez-Vives and Slater, 2005]. More recently, Slater [2009] explained this fundamental illusion as a combination of place illusion — the degree to which you feel that you are in a place (as opposed to watching a place on a screen) — paired with plausibility illusion — the degree to which you believe that the events taking place around you are plausible. The most popular way to currently experience VR is through head-mounted displays, colloquially referred to as VR goggles. Since 2016, a wide range of VR consumer devices have become increasingly available. The lowest range devices include cardboard or plastic goggles that use smartphones as a display and for tracking head motions: Essentially any smartphone can be converted into a VR device at a cost of several dollars. *The New York Times* was a pioneer media outlet in VR use. In November 2015, the newspaper launched a VR smartphone app (https://play.google.com/store/apps/details?id=com.im360nytvr) and shipped 1 million cardboard Google units to their subscribers.

More comprehensive VR solutions provide better quality of experience due to several factors. First, they include external tracking, which allows participants to move around, in contrast to the phone-based solution that currently only detects head rotation. Current smartphone-based VR only tracks head rotation (three degrees of freedom) using the smartphone's accelerometer (smartphones with no accelerometer cannot be used for VR at all). The result is that smartphone-based VR solution users are not expected to move in space; if they do, their motions are not tracked, and individuals often experience nausea, referred to as simulation sickness. Technically, full head tracking that tracks the head's rotation in six degrees of freedom (i.e., both head rotation and head movement) is currently only possible when accompanied by an external tracking sensor (mounted on the ceiling or on walls; separate from the smart device). So-called "inside-out" tracking, based on machine vision technologies, are under development in the industry, so next generations of mobile VR may be able to provide full tracking without external sensors. Another advantage of desktop-based VR systems is that they benefit from greater processing power in the form of dedicated graphics cards that can be added to personal computers.

It is estimated that 6.3 million VR devices were shipped to customers in 2016, not including cardboard and plastic goggles [Durbin, 2017]. While these are very impressive numbers for the early-stage penetration of a new technology, they are far from implying mass worldwide adoption. Nevertheless, VR and AR (augmented reality) devices are expected to eventually hit mass adoption; see below for more on AR. It is impossible to predict market trends, but it is clear that all major tech companies are involved in ambitious efforts to develop next generation devices and applications, which are expected to be launched in the next few years and offer new features. The ambitious goal of these teams is to replace the current paradigm of interacting with computers based on a display keyboard and mouse, which was introduced by Engelbart in the 1960s [Rheingold, 2013].

Most VR content is synthetic, based on 3D models and animation, also known as interactive computer graphics (CGI). An alternative production pipeline, which at present plays a major role in immersive journalism, is 360° videos, which are captured using 360° cameras. Typical setups include at least two wide-angle cameras, and high-end devices may include dozens of cameras. The video feed derived from the multiple cameras then needs to be stitched, albeit this can be done automatically with only minor glitches. The 360° videos are then edited in a process similar to traditional video editing. Using this method, individuals can generate 360° videos, almost as easily as traditional video.

Although 360° videos are similar to traditional videos in some respects, such as that both these technologies allow for the narrative created to be portrayed from multiple angles, there are vital differences in their respective production methods, in the experience they offer, and the underlying principles of cinematic expression they use. Since the camera captures the environment in its entirety, plotting the scene and the shots is significantly dissimilar to that of traditional video, which merely captures motion pictures using digital image sensors. Many of the techniques that can be used by video editors in traditional frame composition are unavailable or irrelevant in VR. Unlike video, where the editor has a high degree of control over the visual experience of the audience, VR participants can turn their heads around using the 360° setting, allowing each participant control of their experience; as a result the editor loses a form of control over what and when the audience member will experience. Arguably, this makes 360° videos more appropriate than traditional video for journalism, since the material is arguably closer to the journalist's original experience and potentially less amenable to manipulation by editors. Can 360° videos be considered a form of VR? Our view is that 360° videos have several interesting properties, such as sensorimotor contingencies and being surrounded by the mediated space, yet they lack properties such as including interactivity and the kinetic ability to negotiate virtual space.

Eventually, the convergence of CGI and video-based VR is expected, but this may take a few more years. Techniques such as volumetric video or dynamic photogrammetry will make it possible to capture a dynamic 3D scene automatically using multiple cameras. Unlike CGI, the visual content in this case is mostly natural and captured by a camera. Unlike 360° videos, the result is a complete 3D model, in which participants can walk around. Capturing a static environment into a 3D model has become quite straightforward and almost automatic: The current challenge is capturing dynamic events. Significant efforts are being made in several application domains, most notably sports broadcasting, with an obvious advantage: Imagine that viewers at home can watch the match from any angle, interactively, or even experience the match as if they were located on or above the sports field. What we are witnessing today are merely the first buds of these technologies, but given the massive industry efforts, we can expect rapid progress.

2. VR Storytelling

However, before considering whether and how VR can be used for storytelling in journalism, we must be aware of the ongoing debate over whether storytelling can be interactive. Hence, while video games seem to have solved the interactivity dilemma [Murray, 1997], there are still some arguments that interactive media has reduced the role of the storyteller to that of a game designer, i.e., designing the environment and the rules, while the narrative emerges from the interaction. According to this view, full interactive VR might actually be less suitable for journalistic storytelling compared to alternative paradigms such as world-building, because in the world of science fiction, world-building is a technique of designing visionary worlds whose cohesive social, geographic, cultural, and alternative features possess a lengthy history [von Stackelberg and McDowell, 2015]. An example is Rilao, an open source project that conjures up a fictional enclave in the Pacific Ocean. This world-building project incorporated parts of the actual cities of Rio de Janeiro and Los Angeles to design the story realm or rather, the DNA, for the Rilao project [von Stackelberg and McDowell, 2015]. Indeed, *The New York Times* senior editor Sam Dolnick commented on the shift from narratives to world building: "In traditional magazine journalism, often somebody comes up with an idea and the editors will say, 'That's a great world, but there's no story.' And now in VR, it feels like it's a little bit flipped. The editors will say, 'Well, that's a neat story. But we really need a world.'" [cited in Robertson, 2016].

As such, linear and non-interactive 360° videos, which are more easily assimilated into journalistic practices, may thus be deemed more appropriate for journalistic storytelling. Nonetheless, an amalgamation between these technologies is seen, as broached by immersive journalism pioneer Nonny de la Pena; while using CGI rather than video, she most often opts for linear, essentially non-interactive VR experiences. Even these linear VR experiences are subject to the challenges induced by assigning participants some freedom: Participants may miss crucial events by incidentally looking in the opposite direction when these events occur.

Despite many years of exploration by the academic and artistic communities [Friedman and Feldman, 2006; Galyean, 1995], our view is that the verdict is still out on whether and how VR can be used for storytelling. While the possibility of creating virtual reconstructions of real events has attracted much attention, it is not clear whether such applications will become mainstream, or what artistic, ethical, and/or professional guidelines would be applicable.

3. Perspective Taking, Empathy, and the Virtual Body

One of the most interesting and powerful means of countenance in VR is the first-person body ownership illusion, which has been applied from neuroscience research to VR. The feeling of owning a body is adaptive and is caused by a human being's ability to relate to their sensory environment. In the original rubber-hand illusion experiment [Botvinick and Cohen, 1998], the participant's real hand is obscured and a rubber arm is placed on a desk, in a plausible location. By tapping on both the real and the rubber hands simultaneously, the experimenter induces in participants a strong illusion that the rubber arm is their own. The illusion is induced by the mismatch between the visual and tactile information entering the brain. It has been shown that this illusion can also be induced by a virtual arm in VR [Slater *et al.*, 2008] (see Figure 1), and even an entire "out-of-body illusion" can be induced [Ehrsson, 2007]. Participants donned a head-mounted display that streamed a video of the viewpoint of a camera behind them, through which they could see the back of their body. Upon being touched on the back, they would see the exact action being replicated on the body in front of them, causing this illusion.

After establishing that VR is suitable to study this illusion, researchers continued to use VR to explore additional virtual body illusions, with the ultimate aim of exposing the underlying neural mechanisms of body ownership, and the extent to which they can be manipulated [Slater *et al.*, 2008, 2009]. Specifically, it has been found that an illusion based on visual-motor synchronization is stronger than an illusion based on visual-tactile synchronization. In other words, virtual body ownership in VR is an effective tool for manipulating the sensation of body ownership.

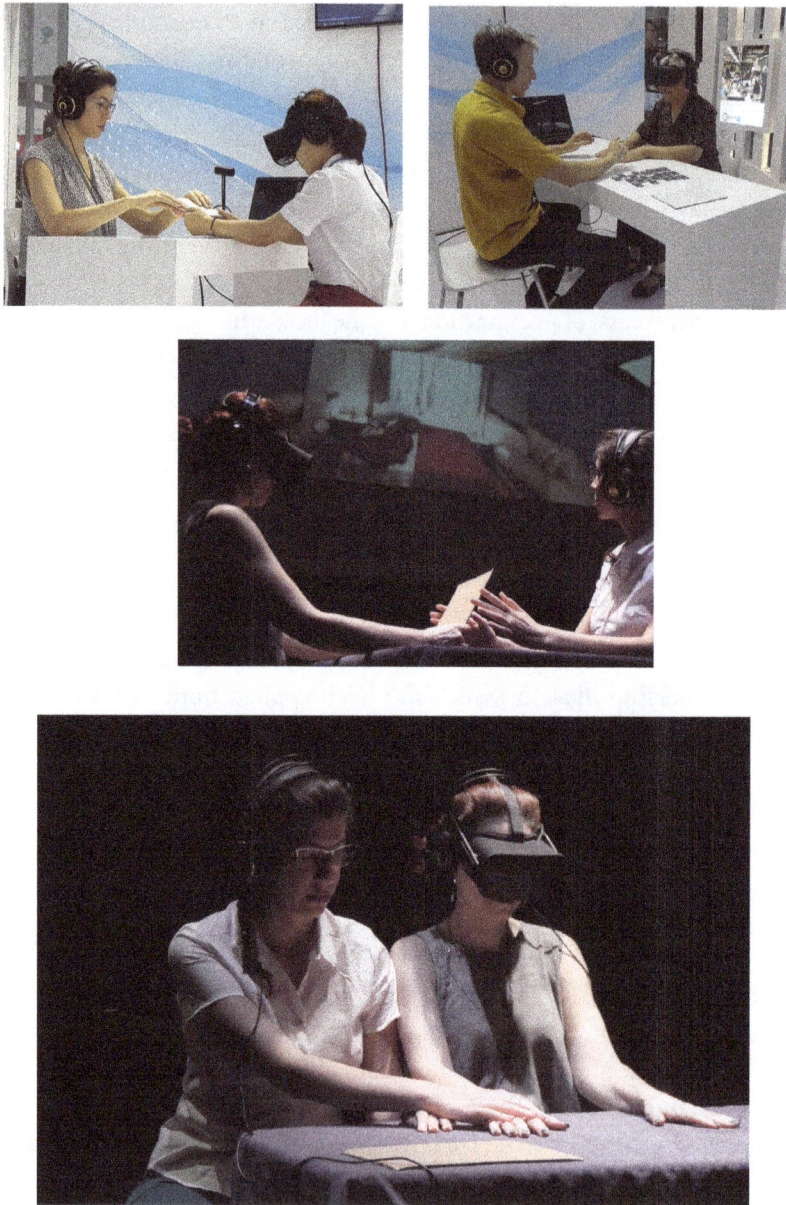

Figure 1.   Screenshots from Time-Body Experiment, a media art installation by artist Daniel Landau, which also served as the framework for a scientific experiment by one of this chapter's co-authors. The VR installation builds on the rubber-hand illusion using a 360° video technique. The participant places his or her hand on the table, and views, from a first-person perspective, a video showing a pair of hands on a table. The hands depict different genders and age groups. The video shows a woman tapping the hands or touching them in various ways. An experimenter touches the real hands of the participant in exactly the same manner at the same time points.

This line of research demonstrated that VR and the body ownership illusion can be used to explore what it is to "become someone else" in a new manner, more visceral than ever. These academic investigations spread from research to popular culture when attendance at one of Slater's VR experiments inspired a young Spanish artist and a group of Barcelona-based artists (BeAnotherLab, retrieved from http://www.themachi-netobeanother.org/) to set up, in 2014, a project entitled "The machine to be another".

The strong public interest in this topic raises the question of whether VR holds the potential to be effectively used in order to allow our audience to "be someone else", and what exactly this means. First, we stress the difference between perspective taking and the body ownership illusion. In perspective taking, you see the scene from different perspectives, or from different points of view; Perhaps you even view yourself from the perspective of another human (in a 360° video) or an avatar (see Figure 2).

Figure 2.   Screenshot from "The Checkpoint", a media art installation by artist Daniel Landau [2015], which also serves as the framework for a scientific experiment by one of this chapter's co-authors. The VR experience is based on a directed scenario that is fictional, but aims at being realistic. The scene describes a pregnant Palestinian woman, accompanied by her husband, on the way to hospital. The couple reaches a checkpoint manned by two Israeli soldiers, who have just received an alert regarding a woman terrorist. The result is a tense event, with both sides apprehensive of the other. The scene is portrayed to participants from different angles: (i) from the perspective of the Palestinian couple, (ii) from the perspective of the Israeli soldiers, and (iii) from a "neutral" wide-angle perspective. In this case, virtual body ownership was not possible, so the director opted to use an over the shoulder camera placement to create a third-person perspective.

In a full body illusion, the sensation is radically different, and consequently the behavioral impact is much stronger. You find yourself inside a virtual body, and the most important aspect of this vestige is the sensorimotor contingencies — you move your hand, and you see the virtual hand move; you move your leg, and you see the corresponding virtual leg move accordingly. Current consumer VR devices lack the technical capacity for full body tracking, and thus preclude a high-quality illusion of body ownership, for the time being.

A small number of research laboratories that have experimented with full body tracking, and make use of the full body ownership illusion, turned to scientifically explore whether we have the proficiency to enable our participants to "become someone else". A range of studies looked at the behavioral and psychological effects of being in alternative bodies, and the results are dramatic. Participants embodied in a child avatar overestimated the size of objects, and had significantly more rapid reaction times in an implicit association test when the self was classified with child-like compared with adult-like attributes [Banakou *et al.*, 2013]. Interestingly, being embodied in a member of a different race has been shown to reverse the in-group bias effect: When embodied in a black virtual body, white participants treat blacks as their in-group and whites become their out-group, as indicated by body mirroring behavior [Hasler *et al.*, 2017]. This reversed in-group bias effect was obtained regardless of participants' level of implicit racial bias. Maister *et al.* [2015] published a recent comprehensive review and proposed a theoretical framework for the psychological impact of virtual re-embodiment.

4. Beyond VR

VR as discussed so far can be considered a subset of a larger family of technologies that includes: (a) VR, which makes you believe you are in an imaginary place; (b) AR, which, makes you believe that some imaginary entities or objects are present with you in the real world [Witt *et al.*, 2016]; and (c) telepresence [Heeter, 1992], which makes you believe you are in a real yet remote location. All three technologies can be delivered to a single participant or to multiple participants simultaneously (creating multi-user environments). AR and telepresence involve technological challenges beyond VR, mostly capturing and understanding the real world. As a result, these technologies may be further down the road, and the opportunities they offer are beyond the scope of this chapter. Unlike VR, which has been available to a wide public since 2016, head-mounted AR and telepresence devices are typically not available to non-professionals, which explains why no practical attempts have been made to harness their potential for journalistic storytelling. AR and telepresence will arguably enable a wider range of applications compared to VR; they are expected to introduce an even more significant disruption to the way we produce and experience mediated content, and the impact of these technologies on journalism is also likely to be dramatic.

5. Immersive Journalism: Early Steps and Current State of the Art

The historic roots of immersive journalism can be traced to the field of newsgames: journalistic storytelling using video games. Newsgames is a subgenre of gaming that was inspired by real situations and conflicts in society. Newsgames, a term coined by Frasca, have been described as a "simulation meets political cartoons" [Treanor and Mateas, 2009] and as tools that "utilize the medium with the intention of participating in the public debate" [Sicart, 2008, p. 27]. Newsgames are thus not merely a form of gaming, but rather a genre of public debate that was formed to illustrate news in an interactive manner. The goal of this type of gaming is not to persuade but rather to illustrate what traditional printed news cannot. Newsgames showcase the role of news in society and the way the news affects various cultures.

A notable example of the transition from newsgames to immersive journalism is Gonne Gitmo [De la Peña and Weil, 2007]. De la Peña, a social activist and journalist, frustrated by the inaccessibility of Guantanamo prison to journalists and by the impossibility of documenting it using traditional tools, reconstructed the prison in the massive multi-user online world Second Life. This virtual world is a non-gaming virtual environment, experienced non-immersively on laptop and desktop computers. Through this fictional experience, participants are taken through several steps of being a prisoner in Guantanamo Bay prison camp. As explained by De la Peña, "We make these pieces because we can put you on the scene, make you feel like you're a witness to an actual event. You're not separated by a television or a screen, you actually feel like you're there" [Schupak, 2015, p. 1].

The fact that many times stories are narrated by visionaries, writers, tech intellects, and design teams raises the question of the journalist's presence in the virtual world. A prime example of the exclusion of a journalist in the VR world is illustrated by "Clouds over Sidra" — a story about Sidra, a 12-year-old girl residing in Zaatari, a Syrian refugee camp in Jordan [Arora and Milk, 2015]. The journalist and camera crew are completely omitted from the VR world in order to focus on the ultimate aim of enabling the participant's presence in the VR world without distractions. The production of this story focuses on the participant's firsthand experience of what Sidra sees, promoting the participant to identify with her on a human level. Such a VR-based storytelling format raises the question of whether the journalists' role in the future will be one that is replaceable by a digital simulation. If this kind of immersive interaction becomes commonplace, the need for investigative writers can be expected to decline as automated machinery gradually takes their place.

De la Peña's first full VR documentary, Project Syria (https://docubase.mit.edu/ project/project-syria/) was triggered by her desire to create news that places the participant in the scene of the actual situation. Along with her creative team of developers, designers, and producers, De la Peña recreated situations in Syria with photorealistic editing and audiovisual recordings. The team gathered photos and videos from Syria and replicated actual people paired with recordings and visuals as seen through their own eyes. The scenes depict typical moments in the war in Syria, including scenes from a bustling street in Aleppo. While a song is playing, a rocket emerges from nowhere and an explosion occurs. In the next scene, a refugee camp is shown with the participant portrayed as a resident of the camp, in order to communicate how it feels to be a refugee forced to flee from his home. Following the Gonne Gitmo project, De la Peña created a short VR piece as an immersive experience illustrating another controversial prison, Abu Ghraib in Iraq, and authored an influential manifesto for the field of immersive journalism [De la Peña *et al.*, 2010].

Importantly, De la Peña's methodology [De la Peña *et al.*, 2010] gives top priority to journalistic principles rather than to sophisticated VR technology. The first stage in her work is always collecting primary sources, mostly still images and audio recordings, from the real world. In the second stage, the scenes are reconstructed in VR, using the original images and sound recordings. Thus, the act of reconstructing the scene in VR is arguably even more authentic than a documentary video, in which editing and postproduction techniques may be used to manipulate the portrayal of events.

Ben Khalifa is a photojournalist and war correspondent who has witnessed the consequences of geopolitical shifts while photographing war-stricken countries. His project "The Enemy" was born of an aspiration to foster world peace by portraying the conflicts in our world. He uses VR to bring participants face-to-face with combatants from three conflict zones: Maras in Salvador, Democratic Republic of the Congo, and Israel and Palestine. He uses room-scale tracking technology to create realistic VR interactions with the reconstructed combatants, who are based on real human combatants. Khalifa's work evokes in participants the question, "Could I be you if I were on the other side?" in an attempt to show that we are all human beings whatever our circumstances.

6. Discussion

The emergence of immersive journalism has opened a portal to an entirely new frame of reference for journalism, one that reshapes the way people view news stories and their production. In contrast to texts or videos viewed on a mobile device, whose impact is fleeting, immersive journalism offers an impactful experience that has the potential to resonate through our entire senses and linger. Through this multifaceted form of media, people are able to place themselves in situations as they would appear in real (palpable)-life.

Ben Khalifa, a war correspondent and photographer, felt that the photos he took barely brought to light the people he captured and therefore sought to strike a chord in people by revolutionizing the way we view stories. Similarly, De la Peña, a social activist and documentarist, searched for a medium that would penetrate audience indifference and create tangible social impact. Both journalists turned to VR as a new medium that potentially overcomes the shortcomings of traditional media — photographs and video. Advertisers were also quick to exploit VR's potential to generate behavioral impact: AT&T, along with Reel FX, a VR company, created a campaign for its mobile network called "It Can Wait". The campaign included, but was not limited to, the placement of VR simulators in flagship AT&T stores, comprising a VR headset that participants wear while seated on a car model. The participant views himself driving in a neighborhood but is maneuvering while text messaging. What they see next follows a stream of dangerous events that could occur had they really been texting in real life. As a result of this project, 10 million individuals pledged to not handle their phones while driving [Shiroishi, 2016].

Is VR an effective tool for persuasion? Anecdotal evidence from these news and advertising projects is joined by accumulating scientific evidence that if its principles are applied correctly, VR can increase audience engagement, and may thus have a stronger impact on opinion change, and possibly also on behavior change. However, the overwhelming majority of the available scientifically validated results are based on one-off experiments in research laboratories on academic campuses. The growing adoption of VR will now allow us to learn much more about the ecological validity of these results, and understand whether VR has a stronger impact on attitudes and behavior than traditional types of media.

As such, the question evolves of whether VR is an "empathy machine". Based on the former, we propose that first-person body ownership illusions hold the potential to be an enticing tool, as they have shown to have significant psychological effects. Nevertheless, we suggest caution. We do not yet know if VR evokes empathy or under what conditions. Evidence that the effects of such "embodied-in-someone-else" VR experiences transfer to and persist in the real world is, as yet, anecdotal. Importantly, none of the present scientific studies attempted to use VR to induce empathy toward a member of an out group in a situation of group conflict. In such a case, it is not unlikely that hostility toward the out group might contradict the effects of VR, and possibly generate undesired effects.

How should we use VR for news storytelling? Our view is that the language of VR is yet to undergo major developments. VR is not an extension of cinema, just as cinema was not an extension of theater. Although many of the techniques available to cinematographers, especially frame composition, are unavailable and irrelevant in VR, VR offers a wide range of new means of artistic expression. Our view is that the language of VR is yet to be defined. This is not unlike the early days of cinema, when directors such as D. W. Griffith were compelled to convince their producers that a close-up makes economic sense. With the increased adoption of VR by the masses, by VR artists, and by producers, we expect to see the artistic language of expression evolve rapidly and assume greater sophistication in the next few years. As a part of this process, we expect the guidelines for immersive journalism to emerge.

References

Arora, G. and Milk, C. (2015). Clouds over Sidra [video file]. Retrieved from https://with.in/watch/clouds-over-sidra/

Banakou, D., Groten, R., and Slater, M. (2013). Illusory ownership of a virtual child body causes overestimation of object sizes and implicit attitude changes. *Proceedings of the National Academy of Sciences*, 110(31), 12846–12851.

Botvinick, M. and Cohen, J. (1998). Rubber hands 'feel' touch that eyes see. *Nature*, 391(756). Retrieved from http://dx.doi.org/doi:10.1038/35784

De la Peña, N., Llobera, J., Pomés, A., Spanlang, B., Friedman, D., Sanchez-Vives, M. V., and Slater, M. (2010). Immersive journalism: Immersive virtual reality for the first person experience of news. *PRESENCE: Teleoperators and Virtual Environments*, 19(4), 291–301.

De la Peña, N. and Weil, P. (2007). Gone Gitmo [video file]. Retrieved from https://docubase.mit.edu/project/gone-gitmo/

Durbin, J. (2017). Report: 6.3 million virtual reality headsets shipped in 2016. *UploadVR*. Retrieved from https://uploadvr.com/report-6-3-million-virtual-reality-headsets-shipped-2016/

Ehrsson, H. (2007). The experimental induction of out-of-body experiences. *Science*, 317(5841), 1048–1048.

Friedman, D. and Feldman, Y. (2006). Automated cinematic reasoning about camera behavior. *Expert Systems with Applications*, 30(4), 694–704.

Galyean, T. (1995). *Narrative Guidance of Interactivity* (Doctoral dissertation). Department of Architecture, Massachusetts Institute of Technology, Cambridge, USA.

Hasler, B. S., Spanlang, B., and Slater, M. (2017). Virtual race transformation reverses racial ingroup bias. *PLoS ONE*, *12*(4), e0174965. Retrieved from http://doi.org/10.1371/journal.pone.0174965

Heeter, C. (1992). Being there: The subjective experience of presence. *Presence: Teleoperators and Virtual Environments*, 1(2), 262–271.

Lombard, M. and Ditton, T. (1997). At the heart of it all: The concept of presence. *Journal of Computer-Mediated Communication*, 3(2). Retrieved from http://jcmc.indiana.edu/vol3/issue2/lombard.html

Maister, L., Slater, M., Sanchez-Vives, M. V., and Tsakiris, M. (2015). Changing bodies changes minds: Owning another body affects social cognition. *Trends in Cognitive Sciences*, 19, 6–12.

Murray, J. (1997). *Hamlet on the Holodeck: The Future Narrative in Cyberspace*. New York: The Free Press.

Rheingold, H. (2013). *Douglas Engelbart's Unfinished Revolution. MIT Technology Review*, 15–17. Retrieved from http://www.technologyreview.com/news/517341/douglas-engelbarts-unfinished-revolution/

Robertson, A. (2016). The New York Times is sending out a second round of Google cardboards. *The Verge*. Retrieved from https://www.theverge.com/2016/4/28/11504932/new-york-times-vr-google-cardboard-seeking-plutos-frigid-heart

Sanchez-Vives, M. V. and Slater, M. (2005). From presence to consciousness through virtual reality. *Nature Reviews Neuroscience*, 6(4), 332–339.

Schupak, A. (2015). *Being There: Is Virtual Reality the Future of Journalism?* Retrieved from https://www.cbsnews.com/news/being-there-is-virtual-reality-the-future-of-journalism/

Shiroishi, B. (2016). *Your Inside Connections: 10 Million Pledges and Why it Matters*. Retrieved from http://about.att.com/inside_connections_blog/ten_million_pledges

Sicart, M. (2008). Newsgames: Theory and design. In S. M. Stevens and S. J. Saldamarco (Eds.), *Entertainment Computing* (pp. 27–33). Berlin, Heidelberg: Springer.

Slater, M. (2009). Place illusion and plausibility can lead to realistic behavior in immersive virtual environments. *Philosophical Transactions of the Royal Society. Series B: Biological Sciences*, 364(1535), 3549–3557.

Slater, M. and Sanchez-Vives, M. (2016). Enhancing our lives with immersive virtual reality. *Frontiers in Robotics and AI*, 3, 1–47.

Slater, M., Perez-Marcos, D., Ehrsson, H., and Sanchez-Vives, M. (2008). Towards a digital body: The virtual arm illusion. *Frontiers in Human Neuroscience*, 2. Retrieved from http://dx.doi.org/10.3389/neuro.09.006.2008

Slater, M., Perez-Marcos, D., Ehrsson, H.H., and Sanchez-Vives, M. V. (2009). Inducing illusory ownership of a virtual body. *Frontiers in Neuroscience*, 3(2), 214–220.

Sutherland, I. (1965). Congress report, 1965. *AORN Journal*, 3(2), 123–147.

Treanor, M. and Mateas, M. (2009). Newsgames: Procedural rhetoric meets political cartoons. In *Proceedings of the Digital Games Research Association* (pp. 1–8). London: Digital Games Research Association.

von Stackelberg, P. and McDowell, A. (2015). What in the world? Storyworlds, science fiction, and futures studies. *Journal of Futures Studies*, 20(2), 25–46.

Witt, L., Kperogi, F., Sinclair, G., Bohrer, C., and Negash, S. (2016). Journalism: How one university used virtual worlds to tell true stories. *International Symposium on Online Journalism*, 6(1), 5–33.

Chapter 8

New journalistic story telling covering conflict zones

Noam Lemelshtrich Latar

Human journalists put their lives at risk when covering many of today's global conflict zones. According to the Committee to Protect Journalists, 107 journalists have been killed since the start of the civil war in Syria in 2013, including 14 deaths in 2016 and 18 in 2017 [https://cpj.org/killed/2017/]. In addition to the physical dangers, the experience of a conflict zone and actual contact with the human suffering create psychological challenges for journalists, as they do for ordinary citizens. In fact, the psychological impact of coverage of the human suffering causes many journalists severe traumatic stress from which they may continue to suffer throughout their lives; Studies show that 28.6% of war correspondents are afflicted with lifetime post-traumatic stress disorder (PTSD) [Feinstein *et al.*, 2002, 2014]. The Journalism School at Columbia University established the Dart Center for Journalism and Trauma (dartcenter.org) to study and help journalists suffering from PTSD, and to prepare journalists for covering war zones.

Recent developments in AI algorithms, telepresence technologies, and remote sensors now enable the collection of data from conflict zones without the need for a journalist to be present in person in the battlefield except in rare cases where such remote telepresence technologies are unavailable. The use of these new technologies can be expected to dramatically change war reporting and save journalists' lives, but can these telepresence technologies satisfy our social and political needs for visual and verbal reporting from battle fields?

1. Telepresence Robots in Conflict Areas

Telepresence robots can now assist journalists who cover war zones or terror events: These robots can cover distances safer and faster, and provide a presence that might not be achieved by a human on site. Indeed, the market for telepresence robots has grown rapidly in recent years: Sales of telepresence robots were estimated at USD 1.4 billion in 2016 and are expected to reach USD 8 billion by 2023 [Tiwari, 2017].

The "Afghan Explorer" (AE), developed by Chris Csikszentmihalyi, director of MIT's Computing Culture, in 2002, was involved in one of the earliest uses of a telepresence robot journalist in war zones "to provide images, sound, and interviews from hostile environments off limits to human reporters" [Wakefield, 2002, para. 2]. The AE traveled on four wheels, used solar energy and GPS navigation, and could be operated by a laptop computer or mobile phone. It could even conduct live interviews with people. As Csikszentmihalyi commented, his robot journalist was expendable: "They can imprison it, shoot it. I don't care. It is just a robot, its feelings can't hurt" [cited in Wakefield, 2002, para. 14]. Csikszentmihalyi was, however, also motivated by his mistrust of human journalists' accounts of what was happening and the control of battlefield information. It is a well-known fact that military generals and strategists of all sides prefer to control the battle information in order to allow them to better manipulate the story to fit their target audiences and defend their war strategies [Lemelshtrich Latar, 2017]. A BBC News Online story about the use of the AE in the war zone predicted that the US military might express strong opposition to the introduction of the AE and the US military's response would be "even more hostile than from the local population" [Wakefield, 2002, para. 2].

The pioneering AE was followed by similar telepresence journalist robots that can be remotely operated by journalists. The Beam system, developed by Suitable Technologies of Palo Alto, California (http//www.suitabletech.com), enables the remote presence of a human journalist at an event, without being there physically. The Beam can be remotely controlled by the user who can conduct interviews in a manner similar to a video conference, yet it allows greater interaction than other robots as it can move around and scan a larger area to discover newsworthy events. The Beam can also interact with other Beams in the area that represent other remote users.

Telepresence robots have also been designed by Double Robotics, which developed a remotely controlled mobile teleconferencing system that enables "conversations to happen anywhere and anytime" (http://doublerobotics.com), and by Anybots, whose robot enables an avatar to represent the journalist from different locations (www.Anybots.com).

2. Drone Journalism

Another form of telepresence data collectors that are becoming very popular in war zones are drones. Drones are unmanned aircraft operated remotely by a human supervisor or, if the mission involves collection of data for the media, by a journalist.

Matt Waite, a professor in the College of Journalism and Mass Communications at the University of Nebraska-Lincoln, was the first to recognize the potential and journalistic value of drones in the mid-2000s when he came across a company that was building an aircraft with a camera on the bottom and an on-board computer that was shooting pictures of the ground. When studying to become a licensed pilot, he realized that the greatest impediment to journalists' use of drones had, all along, been regulatory. In order to help others navigate the complicated process of using drones to do journalism, Waite teamed up with Al Tompkins, the Poynter Institute's senior faculty member for broadcasting and online, and held the first Drone Boot Camp, or drone journalism school. He believed that "Journalists have unique training needs that are different from others who want to use drones in their work. Journalists will need specialized training around privacy concerns that drones raise" [Waite, cited in Simon, 2017].

The Professional Society of Drone Journalists (PSDJ) was established in 2011 in recognition of the increasingly significant contribution that drones make to journalists, and the need to define an ethical, educational, and technological framework and best practices in "investigative, disaster, weather, sports, and environmental journalism" (www.dronejournalism.org).

The PSDJ developed a code of ethics that applies primarily to data collected by aerial photography. One of the major issues that the code addresses is the risk that drones pose to civil or military aviation, especially in view of concerns that reports of near collisions between drones and civil aircrafts in many countries may allow governments that wish to control information to issue a ban or impose restrictions on flying drones. Discussions on the regulation of drones have extended to government agencies in many countries, including the US Federal Aviation Administration (US FAA), and the House of Lords in the UK [Lemelshtrich Latar, 2017].

Drones have gradually found their way into the American journalism scene. According to the official FAA data [Azevedo, 2017], the FAA granted more than 3,000 exemptions that allow commercial users to fly drones, on the condition that their operators have a pilot's license. Some of these exemptions have been issued to news organizations such as CNN, which is one of the early adopters of drone use in news reporting. Television stations in the Cox Media Group, including Atlanta's WSB, Boston's WFXT, and Orlando's WFTV, have also incorporated drones into their coverage, using them to report on news, weather conditions, and feature stories [Azevedo, 2017].

Mullin [2016] claims that the most common use of drones for journalists is taking photos and videos of vast swaths of land from above, when covering stories with large spatial applications, particularly natural or man-made disasters, in which the scope of damage and loss cannot be adequately captured by street-level photography. Aerial visuals, in contrast, can be used to create 3D maps of disaster areas that are combined with data to explain how different sections of a community fared after a storm or war.

An interesting issue concerning drones is whether the use of drones in war zones will "gamify" the news by blurring the line between entertainment and reporting for the journalists using them to collect information [Gibb, 2013]. Not unlike the case of soldiers who operate the drones and make decisions to attack or kill targets when they are far removed from the actual site, without context [Culver, 2012], journalists' use of automated technologies and robots to gather information may distance them from the situation they are covering and from its critical contextual cues.

3. Robotic Snakes

Robot snakes are expected to play an increasing role in gathering data from war zones due to their high maneuverability in small, tight spaces, and their inconspicuous appearance. Many commercial companies and defense agencies including DARPA are sponsoring the research of robotic snakes or snakebots for gathering data and intelligence from dangerous locations on the ground, under water, and in space. Guardian S, for example, was developed by Sarcos to "go where no human can or would", including war zones and poisonous spaces on reconnaissance missions [Brown, 2017].

"Anytime we need data from a location that is dangerous for humans, or where it is difficult for humans to access, the Guardian S is a candidate to gather the data," stated Ben Wolff, chairman and CEO of Sarcos [cited in Brown, 2017, para. 3]. The Guardian S is about four feet long, weighs about 10 pounds, and is equipped with a camera, microphone, and infrared sensors that wirelessly relay video and data to its base. In the near future, Sarcos engineers plan to equip the snake robot with an AI machine learning algorithm that will allow it to make human-like decisions when encountering unexpected situations.

Another robot snake is Eelume Robot, currently under development by the Norwegian University of Science and Technology and other collaborators. The Eelume can operate under water as far down as the sea floor. It can swim (like a real sea snake) or use thrusters for propulsion [Dvorsky, 2016]. Eelume was developed to perform undersea maintenance tasks but can be equipped with surveillance and data gathering sensors. Robot snakes are not, however, limited to the ground or under water: Norwegian researchers are studying possibilities of using snakebots for inspection and maintenance works on the European Space Agency's International Space Station, and in the future they may be routinely used on the Moon and on comets [Lamb, 2017].

4. Artificial Eyes: IoT in Aid of Robotic Journalism

According to Cisco, a global leader in IT and networking, the number of objects connected to the Internet is expected to reach 50 billion by 2020, equal to 6.58 connected devices per person. This ecosystem, commonly known as the Internet of Things or IoT, comprises sensors and devices that are controlled by tiny computers that communicate with each other. In contrast to the use of telepresence robots to cover war zones, which has been limited to newsgathering (primarily visual data), the IoT has implications for two distinct aspects of journalism: newsgathering and consumption.

Two types of connected sensor devices are currently used in conflict zones: "artificial eyes" that are operated from a distance, and wearable sensors that are embedded in the clothing of the journalists or others. The most advanced sensors are "silicon retinas", also known as artificial eyes. "Artificial eyes could be left for years to monitor war zones and outer space … London researchers are beginning a project to explore how artificial eyes — 'silicon retinas' — could be made to function as effectively as the real thing. This could help develop systems to monitor dangerous environments without the need for human intervention" [Lamb, 2017, para. 1]. The introduction of "silicon retinas" into war zones to collect data is a part of an IoT project being developed by Professor Maria Martini of Kingston University, whose aim is to explore how an artificial vision system could become as efficient as a human eye [Lamb, 2017]. According to Martini, "This opens up a world of new possibilities for surveillance and other uses, from robots and drones to the next generation of retinal implants, they could be implemented in small devices where people can't go and it's not possible to recharge the battery. Sensors could be thrown from a plane into a forest and left there for years without any need for human intervention. They could also be particularly useful for collecting footage from dangerous places, such as war zones or even other planets" [cited in Lamb, 2017, para. 11]. Smart devices connected to each other can also be used to provide better context to a story, for example by sourcing data on traffic, weather, population density, or power consumption [Marconi, 2016].

The "maker" nature of the IoT also has implications for the future roles of hacktivists and citizens in journalist practices, both as sources who provide access to stories and data and as technological innovators who affect the dissemination of smart technology by improving open-source elements [Augur, 2016]. Wearable sensors allow individuals to become part of journalistic narratives, and to easily share experiences with others.

5. Can Human Journalists Provide Accurate Reports from Conflict Areas?

In addition to the physical and psychological risks to journalists covering war zones, the quality of journalism itself may be at stake [McMahon, 2010]. Academic research shows that human journalists' coverage of war zones is affected by numerous factors including the harsh conditions they experience in the field, the dramatic human suffering they observe, and the fear of reporting on issues that might place their "hosts" in a negative light, even when they are embedded in combat forces or work as freelance reporters. These conditions cause many journalists to compromise their professional ethics when reporting from war zones, which may lead to inaccurate data [Gibb, 2013] and biased reports. For example, a survey of 159 embedded journalists and journalists who operated freely behind the lines in Iraq found that these journalists covered the war considerably differently: Embedded journalists' stories were more positive while freelance journalists posted stories that tended to be more negative [Fahmy and Johnson, 2007].

Roger Simpson and William Coté of the Dart Center of the Columbia School of journalism wrote a code of ethics for journalists covering violence. In their book *Covering Violence* [2006], which is a guide for ethical coverage of conflict zones, they discuss the ethics of interviewing children and rape cases, and provide guidelines for journalists on how to legally obtain information and how to best conduct an interview, with a special emphasis on traumatic events.

6. Conclusions

Today, stories of devastation and human suffering can be collected by telepresence robots such as drones, embedded sensors, or other remote recording technologies, and it is not inconceivable that journalistic robots of the kind described above will assume an increasingly important role in journalistic practice, and may even transform the very nature of journalistic practice. Human journalists who cover war zones have much to gain by embracing robot journalists and new telepresence technologies as assistants and collaborators. Human journalists and robot journalists can collaborate, for example, by fulfilling different functions at different stages of the journalism process in the coverage of wars, conflicts, and terror events: data collection, data analysis, and composition of the narratives [Lemelshtrich Latar, 2017]. In the data collection stage, robot journalists might help overcome the psychological, physical, and ideological factors that affect and compromise human reporting from the war zones in real time, not to mention preventing the real risk to the lives of the reporters whose stories are not favorable to their "hosts". These AI telepresence recording tools are constantly improving as more "brain" power is added and the efficiency of mobility is increased, and we can expect that the task of obtaining visual data from the field, where journalists' lives are at risk, will be less frequently performed by humans, except in those rare situations that are impenetrable by telepresence technologies.

In the data analysis stage, the robot has the clear advantage of rapid data analysis in a search for insights and relevant visual data, by sifting through the enormous amounts of data that are available and can potentially be used in reporting from conflict zones. Data collected by local government agencies, international organizations, academic researchers, media archives, cellular applications, social networks, and more recently, by sensors embedded all around us, are stored in data silos and can be a treasure trove for real-time war media stories [Lemelshtrich Latar, 2017]. Nonetheless, the human journalist will continue to play an important role in this stage by composing the correct questions for the AI tools: Not only can clever questions lead to clever insights and clever stories, but incorporation of in-depth information on the historical evolution of cultural, ethnic, religious, or economic factors of a conflict in journalistic accounts may assist decision makers involved in conflict resolutions.

In the narrative composition stage, the robot journalist has a clear advantage in rapidly producing first drafts in text format, but AI narrative algorithms still find it virtually impossible to comprehend the constantly changing array of available tools and human news consumption habits. Human creativity and ingenuity is necessary to devise new ways to tell the stories that will adapt to the new journalism era — a complex tapestry of technologies and applications as described in this book.

Clearly, the optimal combination of human and robot journalists over the entire journalistic process can considerably advance journalistic coverage of conflict areas. Mechanical tools will be used to collect visual and verbal data from the field, free of fear or psychological biases, while AI tools applied to huge visual and verbal data silos will help human journalists obtain new insights about the conflicts they cover, which could lead to potentially great stories able to achieve the ultimate aims of war journalism — to reduce human suffering and advance the cause of peace.

References

Augur, H. (2016). Empowering journalists with the Internet of Things, *Dataconomy*. Retrieved from http://dataconomy.com/2016/05/empowering-journalists-internet-things/

Azevedo, M. (2017). Drones give journalists a new way to report news. *Cisco The Network.* Retrieved from https://newsroom.cisco.com/feature-content?type=webcontent&articleId=1851973

Brown, M. (2017). These robotic snakes might soon prevent IEDs from kill-ing soldiers. *Inverse Republicant.* Retrieved from https://www.inverse.com/article/27938-snake-robots-missions-ge-sarcos

Culver, K. B. (2012). Ethics aloft: The pros and cons of journalists using drones. *Public Broadcasting Service Media Shift.* Retrieved from http://www.pbs.org/mediashift/2012/12/ethics-aloft-the-pros-and-cons-of-journalistsusing-drones340.html Cunningham, Pam. (2012, November 19).

Dvorsky, G. (2016). Robotic snakes are the stuff of undersea nightmare. *Gizmodo.* Retrieved from https://www.gizmodo.com.au/2016/04/robotic-snakes-are-the-stuff-of-undersea-nightmares/

Fahmy, S. and Johnson, T. J. (2007). Embedded versus unilateral perspectives on Iraq War. *Newspaper Research Journal*, 28(3), 98–114. Retrieved from http://www.researchgate.net/publication/258421892_Embedded_versus_unilateral_perspectives_on_Iraq_War

Feinstein, A., Audet, B., and Waknine, N. (2014). Witnessing images of extreme violence: A psychological study of journalists in the newsroom. *Journal of the Royal Society of Medicine Open*, 5, 1–7. doi: 10.1177/2054270414533323

Feinstein, A., Owen, J., and Blair, N. (2002). A hazardous profession: War, journalists, and psychopathology. *American Journal of Psychiatry*, 159(9), 1570–1575. Retrieved from http://ajp.psychiatryonline.org/doi/pdf/10.1176/appi.ajp.159.9.1570

Gibb, A. S. (2013). *Droning the story* (unpublished master's thesis). The Faculty of Graduate Studies, University of British Columbia.

Lamb, H. (2017). Artificial eyes could be left for years to monitor war zones and outer space. *E&T.* Retrieved from https://eandt.theiet.org/content/articles/2017/04/artificial-eyes-could-be-left-for-years-to-monitor-war-zones-and-outer-space

Lemelshtrich Latar, N. (2017). Can robot journalists replace human journalists in the coverage of wars? In I. Saleh and T. Knieper (Eds.), *The Visual Politics of Wars* (pp. 171–196). Newcastle upon Tyne, UK: Cambridge Scholars Publishing.

Marconi, F. (2016). Making the Internet of Things working for journalism. *AP Insights.* Retrieved from https://insights.ap.org/industry-trends/making-the-internet-of-things-work-for-journalism

McMahon, C. (2010). Building resilience in the war zone against hidden injury. *Pacific Journalism Review*, 16(1), 39–48. Retrieved from http://www.pjreview.info/sites/default/files/articles/pdfs/pjr16(1)_trauma-mcmahon_pp39-48.pdf

Mullin, B. (2016). Why 2016 could be a breakout year for drone journalism. *Poynter.* Retrieved from https://www.poynter.org/2016/why-2016-could-be-a-brea kout-year-for-drone-journalism

Simon, M. (2017). Watch air swirl around a quadcopter drone's rotors. *Wired.* Retrieved from https://www.wired.com/2017/01/stunning-animation-reveals-air-swirling-around-drone/

Simpson, R. and Coté, W. (2006). *Covering Violence: A Guide to Ethical Reporting About Victims and Trauma*. New York: Columbia University Press. Retrieved from http://dartcenter. org/content/covering-violence-guide-to-ethical-reporting-about-victims-trauma#. VefgphGqpBc

Tiwari, R. (2017). Telepresence robots market worth $8 billion by 2023 says a new research at ReportsnReports. *PRNewswire.* Retrieved from http://www.prnewswire.co.in/news-releases/telepresence-robots-market-worth-8-billion-by-2023-says-a-new-research-at-reportsnreports-629893553.html

Wakefield, J. (2002). Robo reporter goes to war. *BBC News Online.* Retrieved from http://news.bbc.co.uk/2/hi/science/nature/1898525.stm

Chapter 9

Evolution, revolution, or a real game changer? Artificial intelligence and sports journalism

Yair Galily

The introduction of new machinery and technologies has always prompted queries about potential effects on the journalism tradition — its content, its means of production, and its consumption. A quite recent development in the realm of digital journalism, software-generated content, or automatically produced content [Clerwall, 2014], has produced studies that have analyzed and discussed how this technological development is being implemented in newsrooms, its effect on newsrooms [Cottle and Ashton, 1999] and journalism practice [Franklin, 2008; Pavlik, 2000], and how journalists consider this development and its impact on their role as journalists [Linden, 2017; van Dalen, 2012]. The aim of this chapter, however, is to look at the field of sports journalism. Against the specific backdrop of sports journalism's content, means of production, and consumption, the question this chapter will try to answer is whether the recent introduction of automatically produced content is merely another evolutionary stage in the field of sport journalism, or has it triggered a revolution that can be defined as a "game changer", with respect to both production and consumption in this area?

1. Why Sport Journalism?

It is well-documented that sports have been covered by the media for almost 200 years [e.g., Tamir and Galily, 2011]. Over time, sports coverage in the written press has gradually transformed from the final section following (mostly political) news to become one of the media's largest, most focal sections. Despite considerable criticism to which it is subjected — as summarized by the familiar ridicule that it is the "toy department of the news media" — sport reports and information remain important for media organizations because of their popularity with advertisers and audiences [Whannel *et al.*, 2010]. Looking at the broader importance of sport and the cultural importance of communication and sport, Boyle [2013, p. 89] affirms that:

> In many ways, sport matters because of what it tells us about aspects of society rather than specifically about the nature of sporting competition. At its most basic level, sport offers an insight into character, human nature (the best and worst of), and human creativity. It reveals aspects of individual and collective identity and its rich diversity of forms (when does a game become a sport?) allows us to project our own feelings and emotions through a cultural activity either at the "live" event or through mediated sporting discourse. It is the ability of sport to connect with the emotional, often rather than the rationale element within us that makes it so compelling. To take the mundane and elevate it into something more than the sum of its parts is a task that sport can perform. The ability to communicate this individually and collectively is a core part of the enduring appeal of this cultural form.

Furthermore, it is claimed by many that sports play a key role in the commercialization and globalization of the media. Over the years, sports supplements in the written press have grown significantly in number and size and are read almost more than any other newspaper supplement. Indeed, for many, the sports supplement remains the central reason for purchasing a newspaper, notwithstanding the technological developments discussed in this chapter.

Research in the field of sports media has therefore focused a great deal on the reciprocal relations between media and sports. Emphasis has been placed on media content, while somehow neglecting the two poles of the transfer-of-information axis: information producers (responsible for the organizational structure, the processes of recruitment, and the production of sports information distributed by them) and the reading public.

2. The Age of Automated Content

With software automatically producing texts in natural language from structured data, the evolution of natural language generation is dramatically changing traditional news production, yet the area of robotic storytelling is more than 40 years old [Meehan, 1977]: Automatic text summaries have been used in weather forecasts since the 1960s [Glahn, 1970], and in sports, medical, and financial reports since the 1990s [Dörr, 2016]. In recent years, software-generated news has gradually become an integral, albeit small, part of the news-making ecosystem, consequently blurring the boundaries between journalism, computer science, and statistics [Linden, 2017]. "Robot journalism" is a popular but banal conceptualization often illustrated as robots typing on computer keyboards. The proper unifying concept to describe this transformation would be computational journalism, which refers to "forms of algorithmic, social scientific and mathematical processes and systems for the production of news" [Young and Hermida, 2015, p. 381] or, using a more normative definition, "the combination of algorithms, data, and knowledge from the social sciences to supplement the accountability function of journalism" [Hamilton and Turner, 2009, p. 2]. Thus, one can only assert, like Coddington [2015], that computational journalism is concerned with the application of the processes of abstraction and automation to information.

3. Sports and Automated Content

Sports journalism embodies a contradiction. On one hand, over the years, it often been viewed as the "poor relation" within journalism, allegedly devoid of the integrity that journalists often like to associate with their profession. Sports journalism has been considered a "soft" form of journalistic practice, lacking the precision or credibility of other forms of "hard" journalism. Sports journalism has been traditionally viewed as an uncritical booster and promoter of sports and its culture rather than a field that challenges and calls for the accountability of the powerful organizations and individuals in the world of sports. More often than not, sports journalism posed the easy and banal questions, rather than the penetrating and pertinent ones [Boyle, 2017]. To Hutchins and Boyle [2017], variations in the practices and norms of contemporary sport journalism are related to widespread transformations across the news industries, as organizations scramble to find sustainable structures and business models. Under the conditions fostered by industrial capitalism and mass communications for much of the twentieth century, news media came to exercise longstanding power by the accumulation of a putatively objective authority built from the systematic administration of news production and the applied expertise of journalists, thereby ensuring the reliability and timeliness of reports. Since technological determinism needs to be coupled with acknowledgement that organizational structure and occupational practices shape the ways in which new technology is adopted and with what effects, it is argued that that human action shapes technology [Linden, 2017].

According to the Associated Press (AP), robo-journalism will create new jobs in the newsroom — potentially bringing in people with different and more diverse skill sets. Heavily dependent on data, robo-journalism can be seen as part of the evolution of data journalism, a genre that has brought welcome diversity to journalism. Other potential benefits include freeing up journalists to do more investigative work and analysis, where human input is essential. At the same time, however, it is argued that robo-journalism might not work equally well in all fields, which is why most efforts are currently focused on relatively formulaic genres such as business/earnings reporting and sport, where journalists can produce templates and computers fill in the gaps. Sports journalism, and baseball in particular, has been considered an ideal domain for computerization and automated journalism because of the wealth of available statistics, the use of prescribed templates and styles, and advanced predictive models in sports reporting [van Dalen, 2012]. Moreover, the training required to ensure the quality of robot-produced texts is expensive and time-intensive, and is feasible in sports journalism due to the relatively high volume of stories.

The introduction of algorithms to automatically generate content from structured data has shaken up the journalism industry — most especially since the AP, one of the world's largest and most well-established news organizations, has started to automate the production of its quarterly corporate earnings reports. Once developed, not only can algorithms create thousands of news stories for a particular topic, they also do it more quickly, cheaply, and potentially with fewer errors than any human journalist. The leading natural language generation technology companies in the United States, Automated Insights and Narrative Science, were born from attempts to generate game recaps automatically.

In 2016, AP attracted wide media coverage when it announced its collaboration with Automated Insights to provide automated game recaps for Minor League Baseball, after AP's sports division had spent a year testing the software to ensure that the Minor League write-ups it produced made sense for fans [McCormick, 2016]. In 2006, AP had used human reporters to cover some Minor League games, but was unable to provide a full account of teams and leagues: By using Automated Insights' software and MLBAM's data, the AP can now report on games that would be impossible to cover without a staff of hundreds of dedicated journalists.

4. The Sporting Angles

Speed and accuracy are two important advantages of and opportunities for automated content creators [Radcliff, 2016]. "… not only can algorithms create thousands of news stories for a particular topic, they also do it more quickly, cheaply, and potentially with fewer errors than any human journalist" [Graefe, 2016, p. 498]. Also, according to Radcliff, technologies don't make the same mistake twice provided there's a human to help train them, like the Norwegian News Agency that successfully automated reporting of football matches in 2016.

Another related issue is ethics and honesty. Clerwall [2014] found that a small group of readers could not reliably determine whether a sports article was written by a human or a robot. Those assigned the automated article found it trustworthy and informative, although a bit boring. Assuming news agencies are transparent and keeping an ethics code, they do have to be honest with their readers.

5. Journalists Are Not Dead Yet! or, How to Remain Artisans in an Era of Automated Content Production?

Journalists have an obvious stake in robo-journalism, but other relevant and powerful social groups also have legitimate interests in automated news: publishers, news managers, developers, media executives, advertisers, the general audience or specific groups within it, producers of data, as well as information brokers who mediate between data producers and users. Government agencies and regulators such as data protection agencies or financial authorities also have their own concerns about the impact of automatically produced content on society in general or on specific practices [Linden, 2017]. However, in line with Winner, I would argue that innovation in technology is a "multicentred, complex process" that creates a "spectrum of possible technological choices, alternatives and branching points" [Winner 1993, p. 366]. Thus, like many other professions in the media sphere, sport journalists will be compelled to adjust to the new reality but by no means will they disappear.

Transparency, creativity, and inclusivity encapsulate the future of journalism. As Wyde [2015] argued, the contemporary drive toward co-operation, cultural awareness, and tolerance will be invaluable in the journalistic sphere. In addition, technological advances will and are currently allowing an unprecedented surge of creativity in the industry, where journalists are finding ever more diverse and fascinating ways to tell their stories. Journalists can use technology to produce better quality articles, much faster. Simple facts can be checked instantly and stories no longer have to consist of plain text, with one or two images. Journalists can use a variety of media to create a lively story, which will in turn engage readers quicker and more easily than a page of cramped text. Although the story itself will still be the backbone of journalism, there will be a greatly increased scope for creativity. If we can imitate Harry Potter's *Daily Prophet*'s moving pictures in advertising on the Tube, for example, it must surely be possible to animate news stories while people are waiting for their train.

Another source of confidence in the professional future of human journalists is the fake news phenomenon. According to Nic Newman, currently a Visiting Fellow at the Reuters Institute for the Study of Journalism and the author of 2017 Digital News: Essential Data on the Future of News:

> … because of fake news, the general public has come to the realization that journalism doesn't come for free. There is good journalism, there is bad journalism, and there is quality journalism which cannot be found everywhere, it is actually quite scarce. It might be something people need to pay for. The increasing pollution of our news environments, which is I think is what is going on, is creating a situation where there is an opportunity for quality news brands or brands that have something to say to actually charge for their either directly or through a creative approach to advertising in the marketplace. I think this is the ray of hope I take from the whole "fake news" debacle [Newman, 2016].

Platforms like Google and Facebook are examples of recent additions to the media ecosystem whose data selection procedures are little known by the public. In addition, these platforms' reliance on algorithmic curation has endowed these procedures with a certain opacity that makes it even more difficult for the public to devise strategies to successfully identify bias, which many skilled (human) journalists are trained to find. Concerns surrounding data ambivalence and limitations in bias detection converge with a deep crisis in the cultural authority of knowledge and low trust in the media as an institution. In an ongoing research project on news consumption, Pablo Boczkowski, professor and director of the Program in Media, Technology, and Society at Northwestern University, and his collaborators found that the same news item is attributed a higher level of credibility if it is shared by a contact on a social media platform than if it is read directly on the originating news site. When asked about this difference, interviewees say it is because they often distrust the media since they are inherently biased, while their default stance toward their social media contacts is based on trust [Fletcher *et al.*, 2015].

Technology is also creating new forms of employment for journalists. The Internet and digital media have created conditions that have prompted the emergence of a new type of work arrangement — entrepreneurial journalism. This differs from "freelance" journalism, in which journalists sell their labor to multiple news organizations on a contract rather than employment basis. As entrepreneurial journalists, journalists establish their own small and medium enterprises to produce content, develop their own distribution mechanisms through websites and blogs, and syndicate their content to other firms [Rottwilm, 2014]. According to Rottwilm, the convergence process, multi-skilling, the need to integrate digital network technologies, and a new producer–consumer relationship have become the most serious challenges for journalism today, including a diluted sense of professional identity caused by the expansion of journalistic work to include consultancy and entre/intrapreneurship. The precise nature, extent, and consequences of these changes are still poorly understood, partly because empirical research on the changing nature of journalistic work and journalistic labor is still limited, and partly because scholarship in journalism and the media has not always engaged directly with the broader literature in economics, sociology, and management.

6. The [Human] Advantage in Sports Journalism

Indeed, sports journalism is becoming progressively complementary, yet there is still a need for all forms of it on a huge variety of platforms. Many sports devotees are no longer pleased with a single source of information: they desire blogs, tweets, and continuous updates, but at the same time they also want lengthier documentaries and crafted narratives.

Paradoxically, rapidly growing automated technology has highlighted the human advantage of telling the story in the sporting world. New technologies created by start-up companies allow reporters/commentators to build new forms of visual stories that will be very difficult for a robot to emulate, as AI is still unable to *combine* visual technologies to build an interesting interactive story. In the past decade, many high-technology companies (Scidel, PVI, SportVision, Replay-technologies [recently acquired by Intel], and Orad, to name just a few) have successfully developed tools that enhance the viewing experience by combing several visual technologies. Such products, initially used in the 2000 Sydney Olympics, allow the superimposition of real-time 3D graphic elements onto the playing field. By analyzing the image on the screen, the system extracts the camera's capabilities, such as pan, tilt, zoom, and focus, so that every camera movement is analyzed in real time and the inserted graphic element can be applied. The end result is that the virtual element is immersed into the real environment as if it were a real physical object, regardless of the camera's movements. For example, when viewers had a hard time keeping track of the fast-moving puck in hockey games, the FoxTrax system (https://en.wikipedia.org/wiki/FoxTrax) was used to visually highlight the puck on-screen and display a trail when the puck was moving rapidly. With more and more cameras being used, super slow-motion cameras and split-second replays from different angles have almost become a standard. Real-time graphics linked with statistics collection systems help commentators to better analyze and visualize the game and help the (often confused) spectators to understand it. As a result, live sports graphics have gone far beyond simply displaying the score and the game's clock: Rosters, fixtures, tables, tickers, and many other graphical data have been integrated with statistic collection systems and databases, allowing real-time player-tracking applications and visualization of the collected records such as distance covered, "heat maps", and other stimulating but rather distracting data.

Orad's virtual graphics superimposed on the playing field have also changed the way home viewers consume sports. Orad's first-down lines have become an integral part of many American football productions, while soccer broadcasts now include virtual offside lines, speed, and distance measurements. These, together with the world record dynamic line during swimming and athletic events, all enhance and enrich the viewing experience, accompanied by a live commentating story-teller.

FreeD™ is another recent technology that captures reality as a true 3D image comprised of 3D "pixels" that faithfully represent the fine details of the scene. This information is stored as a database, which can then be tapped to render any desired viewing angle from the detailed information collected. Replay-technologies' freeD releases storytelling from the constraints of the placement of a physical camera and lens, granting a freedom of viewing that has almost endless possibilities. Such a system allows producers and directors to create "impossible" camera views at any given moment in time.

7. Conclusions

Did a robot write this chapter? No, but it might have …

Despite the difficulty in analysis, the profession of journalism has become a focal object of sociology research, and solid agreement has developed on the number of dimensions that compose the picture of ideal journalism [Singer, 2004]. Along this chapter we explored whether the recent introduction of automatically produced content is merely another evolutionary stage in the field of sport journalism, or it has triggered a revolution that can be defined as a "game changer" in relation to both production and consumption, in this area.

The availability of data feeds, the demand for news on mobile devices, and advances in algorithms are helping to make automated journalism more prevalent [Thurman *et al.*, 2017]. Thus, it is both practical and reasonable to worry that automation will either cause or be used as an excuse for job cuts and dismissal of journalists. However, where journalism jobs have been disappearing, the reasons are to be found in changing consumer behaviors and media business models, not in automation, at least not so far [Linden, 2017]. According to AP managing editor, Lou Ferrara [2016]:

> We are going to use our brains and time in more enterprising ways during earnings season. Rather than spending a great deal of time focusing on the release of

earnings and hammering out a quick story recapping each one, we are going to automate that process … Instead, our journalists will focus on reporting and writing stories about what the numbers mean and what gets said in earnings calls on the day of the release, identifying trends and finding exclusive stories we can publish at the time of the earnings reports … This is about using technology to free journalists to do more journalism and less data processing, not about eliminating jobs [cited in Colford, 2014].

The Associated Press is a case in point. It describes itself as "one of the largest and most trusted sources of independent newsgathering, supplying a steady stream of news to its members, international subscribers and commercial customers." The winner of 51 Pulitzer Prizes, its members include about 1,400 daily US newspapers and thousands of television and radio broadcasters. In addition to content, the company is known for style. AP Style is the definitive writing standard for journalism and for many other fields. AP identified opportunities in automation with Wordsmith, a platform developed by Automated Insights, which uses natural language generation to turn data into a written, plain-language narrative. Wordsmith transforms earnings data from Zacks Investment Research or Major league baseball into publishable AP stories in a fraction of a second. The Wordsmith team even specifically configured the natural language generation engine to write in AP style.

As a result, AP now produces 3,700 quarterly earnings stories — a 12-fold increase over its manual efforts. The stories retain the same quality and accuracy that readers expect from any of AP's human-written articles. Aside from an explanatory note at the bottom of the story, there is no evidence they were written by an algorithm [AutomatedInsights, 2017].

The world is changing and progress, in large shapes and sizes such as robotic and automated content generators, are here to stay. As Smith and Anderson [2014, p. 6] explain:

Robots and AI [artificial intelligence] make compelling stories for journalists, but they are a false vision of the major economic changes. Journalists lost their jobs because of changes to advertising, professors are threatened by MOOCs [massive open online courses], and store salespeople are losing jobs to Internet sales people. Improved user interfaces, electronic delivery (videos, music, etc.), and more self-reliant customers reduce job needs. At the same time someone is building new websites, managing corporate social media plans, creating new products, etc. Improved user interfaces, novel services, and fresh ideas will create more jobs.

Similarly, the case of the Associated Press and baseball, and the practices of many other news agencies in the field of sports, illustrates the game-changing nature of automated journalist technologies. Journalists, like many others, believe that auto-mated journalism will become more common, as the depth, breadth, specificity, and immediacy of information become increasingly available. While some news organiza-tions and consumers may benefit, such changes create new ethical and societal con-cerns, and, perhaps counter-intuitively, may increase the need for skills that human journalists embody, such as news judgment, curiosity, and skepticism [Thurman *et al.*, 2017]. Finally, as Daminan Redcliff, professor in journalism at the University of Oregon clearly predicts: "The robots are coming, but depending on the algorithm, the revolution may not be automatically published …".

References

AutomatedInsights. (2017). Retrieved from https://automatedinsights.com/case-studies/associated-press

Boyle, R. (2013). Reflections on communication and sport: On journalism and digital culture. *Communication & Sport*, 1(1–2), 88–99.

Boyle, R. (2017). Sports journalism: Changing journalism practice and digital media. *Digital Journalism*, 5, 493–495.

Clerwall, C. (2014). Enter the robot journalist: Users" perceptions of automated content. *Journalism Practice*, 8(5), 519–531.

Coddington, M. (2015). Clarifying journalism's quantitative turn: A typology for evaluating data journalism, computational journalism, and computer-assisted reporting. *Digital Journalism*, 3(3), 331–348.

Colford, P. (2014). A leap forward in quarterly earnings stories. *Associated Press*. Retrieved from https://blog.ap.org/announcements/a-leap-forward-in-quarterly-earnings-stories

Cottle, S. and Ashton, M. (1999). From BBC newsroom to BBC newscentre: On changing technology and journalist practices. *Convergence*, 5(3), 22–43.

Dörr, K. N. (2016). Mapping the field of algorithmic journalism. *Digital Journalism*, 4(6), 700–722.

Fletcher, R., Radcliffe, D., Levy, D. A., Nielsen, R. K., and Newman, N. (2015). *Reuters Institute Digital News Report 2015: Supplementary Report*. Oxford: Reuters Institute for the Study of Jerusalem, University of Oxford.

Franklin, B. (2008). The future of newspapers. *Journalism Practice*, 2(3), 306–317.

Glahn, H. R. (1970). Computer-produced worded forecasts. *Bulletin of the American Meteorological Society*, 51(12), 1126–1131.

Graefe, A. (2016). *Guide to Automated Journalism*. New York: Columbia University Academic Commons.

Hamilton, J. T. and Turner, F. (2009). Accountability through algorithm: Developing the field of computational journalism. A report from the Center for Advanced Study in the Behavioral Sciences, Summer Workshop, July 27–31.

Hutchins, B. and Boyle, R. (2017). A community of practice: Sport journalism, mobile media and institutional change. *Digital Journalism*, 5(5), 496–512.

Linden, C. G. (2017). Decades of automation in the newsroom: Why are there still so many jobs in journalism? *Digital Journalism*, 5(2), 123–140.

McCormick, R. (2016). AP's robot journalists are writing about Minor League Baseball now. *The Verge*. Retrieved from https://www.theverge.com/2016/7/4/12092768/ap-robot-journalists-automated-insights-minor-league-baseball

Meehan, J. R. (1977). TALE-SPIN, an interactive program that writes stories. In *Proceedings of the fifth International Joint Conference on Artificial Intelligence (INCAI'77)* (pp. 91–98). San Mateo, CA: Morgan Kaufmann. http://ijcai.org./search.php

Newman, N. (2016). *The Future of Journalism is Not All Doom and Gloom*. Interview. Retrieved from: https://medium.com/global-editors-network/the-future-of-journalism-is-not-all-doom-and-gloom-heres-why-365ed8003899

Pavlik, J. (2000). The impact of technology on journalism. *Journalism Studies*, 1(2), 229–237.

Radcliff, D. (2016). The upsides (and downsides) of automated robot journalism. Retrieved from http://mediashift.org/2016/07/upsides-downsides-automated-robot-journalism/

Rottwilm, P. (2014). *The Future of Journalistic Work: Its Changing Nature and Implications*. London: Reuters Institute for the Study of Journalism.

Singer, D. G. (2004). *Television, Imagination, and Aggression: A Study of Preschoolers*. London: Routledge.

Smith, A. and Anderson, J. (2014). AI, robotics, and the future of jobs. *Pew Research Center*, 6. http://www.fusbp.com/wp-content/uploads/2010/07/AI-and-Robotics-Impact-on-Future-Pew-Survey.pdf

Tamir, I. and Galily, Y. (2011). The human factor in the historical development of the media: Israeli sports pages as a case study 1. *The International Journal of the History of Sport*, 28(18), 2688–2706.

Thurman, N., Dörr, K., and Kunert, J. (2017). When reporters get hands-on with robo-writing: professionals consider automated journalism's capabilities and consequences. *Digital Journalism*. http://www.tandfonline.com/doi/abs/10.1080/2167 0811.2017.1289819

van Dalen, A. (2012). The algorithms behind the headlines: How machine-written news redefines the core skills of human journalists. *Journalism Practice*, 6(5–6), 648–658.

Whannel, G., Boyle, R., and Rowe, D. (2010). Delight in trivial controversy? Questions for sport journalism. In S. Allan (Ed.), *Routledge Companion to News and Journalism* (pp. 245–255). London: Routledge.

Winner, L. (1993). Upon opening the black box and finding it empty: Social constructivism and the philosophy of technology. *Science, Technology, and Human Values* 18(3), 362–378.

Wyde, R. (2015). What is the future of journalism? *The Guardian*. Retrieved from https://www.theguardian.com/media/2015/apr/15/what-is-the-future-of-journalism

Young, M. L. and Hermida, A. (2015). From Mr. and Mrs. outlier to central tendencies: Computational journalism and crime reporting at the Los Angeles Times. *Digital Journalism*, 3(3), 381–397.

Chapter 10

Cybernetics and the new storytelling of government decision making in the age of AI

Noam Lemelshtrich Latar

"There's a great phrase, written in the '70s: The definition of today's AI is a machine that can make a perfect chess move while the room is on fire".

[Knight, 2017a, para. 4]

1. Introduction

Journalists who cover political and social issues in the coming Big Data and Artificial Intelligence (AI) decades must have a general understanding of systems theories and analysis if they are to become significant participants in the new storytelling of government decision-making processes in the age of AI. They must understand organizational behavior, how the different organs of a social system interact with and affect one another, and they must understand how decisions are made and communicated among the different organs of a system. They must understand how a system's interactions with its political and social environments affect its ability to achieve its stated goals.

As the amount of data generated by organizations and their relevant environments has become virtually unlimited in the Big Data age, human journalists will lose the competition with their robot competitors without some basic understanding of systems theory and the new social dynamics. Today's private and governmental organizations use algorithms that are programed to sift through vast volumes of data to understand and analyze the digital social and organizational dynamics, to discover hidden insights and trends, and make decisions automatically. In this chapter, we discuss cybernetic theory, which offers a useful framework for system analysis by focusing on how systems are governed, and how information flows among a system's organs and between a system and its relevant environments. Cybernetic theory facilitates investigations of systems and organizations, allowing predictions of their chances to achieve their stated goals and their chances of survival in changing environments. Human journalists must understand how decision making in these organizations affects these processes if they are to protect democracy and citizens' well-being. Robot journalists cannot be entrusted with this crucial mission.

2. Big Data and Bureaucracy

Social organizations, especially governmental organizations, operate as bureaucracies, which are defined as "large public and private organizations with hierarchical structures and a set of elaborate rules and processes" [Solove, 2004, p. 38]. According to Max Weber, one of the founders of sociology, a bureaucracy is capable of attaining the highest degree of efficiency as it is "formally a most rational means of exercising authority over human beings" [Weber, 1922/1978, p. 223]. Yet Weber also describes bureaucracies as "dehumanized" and devoid of sensitivity to unquantifiable human emotions and needs. Today, bureaucracies' aspiration to achieve maximum efficiency depends on the collection of information in data silos and the development of data analytics tools adapted to rules, regulations, and goals of each bureaucracy. AI algorithms enhance a bureaucracy's efficiency potential by integrating machine learning tools in bureaucratic decision-making processes, which allows the system to learn from its mistakes and experience. Cybernetic theory offers a useful framework for journalists who wish to understand bureaucracies and their pitfalls.

3. Cybernetics

Cybernetics, the science of self-regulation [Wiener, 1949], contributes a unique theoretical perspective for assessing whether a given social bureaucracy is being governed in a manner that supports its adaptiveness to changing environments and the attainment of its social objectives, or whether it is heading towards chaos. The notion of feedback plays an important role in the theory of cybernetics, which, when applied to social systems, gives freedom of expression a new context and important meaning: Where individuals fear expressing themselves freely, the feedback that the system collects about its internal and external environment is inaccurate, creating false status reports that adversely affect decision making.

The cybernetic method analyzes the dynamics of information flows within the different components of a social system and the effectiveness of its decision-making processes, while relying on quantitative measurements of all parts of the system along predefined indices. Cybernetics focuses on these major questions: Can a system adapt fast enough to changes in the environment? Can it automatically find a new equilibrium with the changing environment? One of the aims of the cybernetic model is to predict the future behavior of social systems, test the quality of their decision making, and thus facilitate the development of corrective policies [Lemelshtrich Latar, 1990]. "Both AI and cybernetics are based on binary logic, and both rely on the same principle for the results they produce: intent. The logical part is universal; The intent is culture-specific" [Krikke, 2017].

There are three basic assumptions behind Wiener's cybernetic model: (a) Control is a most important process in nature; (b) An organization's survival depends on its ability to process information effectively; and (c) Biological, mechanical, and social systems process information in a similar way.

According to modern theories of decision making, a good decision depends on accurate and timely information. Information must be accurate in terms of correctly describing the state of affairs at the time of decision making. That a distorted picture of reality could lead to incorrect decisions is especially true in social, political, and economic decision making: Social revolutions, economic crises, and even wars have been caused by an absence of accurate information.

According to the cybernetic model, a decision is made after the system measures the deviation of the present state of affairs from the system's goals or desired state of affairs. The purpose of the decision is to diminish and eventually eliminate this deviation, to attain the desired state of affairs. It is possible to measure deviations from goals only if the system has defined goals for itself and if accurate information about the state of the system exists at the time of decision making. Today, the process of obtaining true, accurate, quantified information on the environment — feedback — faces multiple challenges including political censorship, "fake news", political fear, and lack of freedom of the press or freedom of expression.

4. The Cybernetic Model

The cybernetic model is illustrated in Figure 1. The main elements of this model are:

Sensors: Sensors collect raw feedback from the system's environment. In the case of a social system, the sensors must be able to detect all the potential environmental elements that might affect the system's behavior. Today, such sensors are being embedded in all the "things" surrounding us, creating the "Internet of Things" (IoT).

The Cybernetic Model

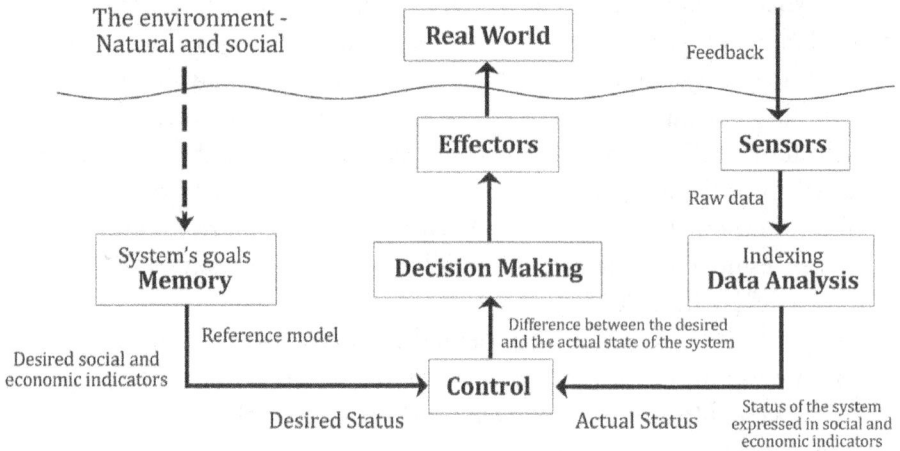

Figure 1.   The cybernetic model.

Indexing: Indexing is used to transform the huge amounts of raw data collected by the sensors into numerical social and economic indicators and indices (such as the standard of living index, rate of unemployment, economic growth, and average income). Meaningful feedback must also be able to detect complex aspects of communications and content such as religious sentiments, self-esteem of citizens, citizen motivation to participate in the social system, political apathy, stereotypes, socialization, cultural integration, escapism, and institutional apathy, to name a few. Together, these social indicators describe the state of the system at a given time.

Control: Once the current state of the system is quantified — or transformed into indices — this information is transferred to an element of control, where the current state of affairs is then compared to the system's desired state of affairs: its short- and long-term goals, expressed in identical units. The control function identifies deviations of the current state from the desired state, and transfers this information to the system's decision-makers. For a system to operate as a cybernetic system it must have clear goals. Without predefined goals, the system is unable to measure the difference between the desired state of affairs and the current state of affairs or provide accurate information for corrective decision making.

Memory: A system's memory comprises all the data silos that store the feedback that the system continually collects, the system's stated goals, and all past decision-making processes. In the age of Big Data, the volume of stored information is huge and grows exponentially.

Decision making: The decision-making function's task is to make decisions to reduce or eliminate the deviations from the system's desired state of affairs and bring the system closer to attaining its goals. In an efficient rational system, decision-makers study past decisions to learn from previous errors. Therefore, a true cybernetic system improves with experience. The decision-making body (or government) instructs the implementation bodies to implement the decisions.

Positive and negative feedback loops: Cybernetic theorists identify two types of feedback loops: a negative feedback loop and a positive feedback loop. The descriptors "negative" and "positive" have no relation to valence, but rather refer to processes with and without controls, respectively. When journalists analyze the behavior of a social organization, identification of feedback loops and their consequences is an important step in understanding the organization's behavior.

A negative feedback loop describes a system with goal-directed behavior. A cybernetic system, if properly designed, is a negative feedback system, which means that the system has built-in control elements that discover deviations from the system's stated goals and make corrective decisions to correct these deviations. In contrast, social systems without stated goals are characterized by positive feedback loops. Examples of such systems are an arms race, social unrest, and inflation. In these kinds of situations, the system's behavior resembles a snowball effect.

Equilibrium: Equilibrium is defined as the situation in which a cybernetic system detects no difference between the current state of affairs and the desired state of affairs (the system's goals). From a cybernetic point of view, equilibrium is the state in which goals have been achieved, yet at this point the system automatically resists all change. Attaining equilibrium in a cybernetic system can lead to the inhibition of social change due to the inherent conflict between the structural rigidity typical of cybernetic systems that strive toward equilibrium and the flexibility that social organizations need in order to adapt to internal and external changes.

5. Sociocybernetics and General Systems Theory

Social scientists have recognized the importance of theories developed in the scientific field of General Systems Theory (GTS) for understanding social and political processes, which is a main arena of journalistic practice. According to GTS, systems can be either controlled (cybernetic) or uncontrolled. In controlled systems, the *detector* function senses information, the *selector* function filters information according to the system's decision-making rules, and the *effector* function carries out transactions with other systems [Kuhn, 1974]. Furthermore, the theory posits that the efficiency of political decision making and social and political behavior are directly affected by the synergy and mutual effects of all the elements in a social system and the quality of information flows among them.

In 1980, in response to a widespread recognition of the importance of GTS, the International Sociological Association's (ISA) Research Committee 51 (RC51) along with 50 other social research groups, established the research field of socio-cybernetics, which is an interdisciplinary field that combines social science, political science, economics, statistics, mathematics, and anthropology. Sociocybernetics can be defined as "systems science in sociology and other social sciences". It is a science because sociocybernetics is not limited to theory but includes applications, empirical research, methodology, axiology (ethics and value research), and epistemology. In general use, systems theory and cybernetics are frequently interchangeable or appear in combination.

6. Social Development Theory

Arab-Ogly, a Czech scientist, developed a theory of social development based on the cybernetics concepts [Arab-Ogly, 1958; Ford, 1966], which highlights the synergy between cybernetics and social dynamics. According to social development theory, the very survival of all social systems is conditional upon the introduction of automation and cybernetics. Some of the major premises of this important theory include:

(1) Society strives for systematization, and is directed towards increased levels of organization and regulation.
(2) Each new stage in social development results in a more complex form of organization, which aims to result in increased orderliness. Social organizations' inherent drive to increased complexity is coupled with the development of methods to simplify their governing procedures. Today, the tendency toward increased complexity is manifest in the accumulation of information in data silos (or Big Data), while the aspiration for simplification finds expression in the development of new algorithms to manage these data silos.
(3) As healthy organizations thrive, their increased level of complexity provides the organizations with increasingly sophisticated AI-based tools to adapt to changes in their environments and ensure their survival.
(4) Social activity aims to transform the environment in ways that satisfy human needs. As the environment is transformed, members of the social system adapt ideologically to these changes.

(5) The variety of methods available to society to adapt to environmental changes is a direct function of the amount of information available to society, assuming it possesses efficient information retrieval methods.

(6) There are no upper bounds on the level of complexity of a social system. Therefore, increased complexity must always be accompanied by the development of efficient ways to handle this complexity, which is possible only through automation.

7. AI and Cybernetics

AI algorithms are being introduced into all the elements that comprise political bureaucracies and decision-making processes, as described by the cybernetic model. Algorithms are being introduced into government decision-making processes in such fields as criminal justice, healthcare, welfare and education. Relevant citizen profiles are introduced into the decision algorithms and affect the outcomes. For example, in criminal cases, the profiles of the offenders are introduced in some states in the US in order to predict their future behavior. The algorithms set a score for each individual based on past behavior and demographic attributes, including skin color, and this score affects the sentences. This was studied by a group of ProPublica journalists who concluded that "There is a software used across the country to predict future criminals and it is biased against blacks" [Angwin *et al.*, 2016]. This is a prime example of human journalism that focuses on the study of the dangers of AI to the social systems. Journalists must be aware of these new trends, which can have great benefits but also could be dangerous due to some basic flaws in these algorithms. The algorithms are and will continue to be written by human beings, at least in the foreseeable future. People are biased, and their biases (specifically the biases of algorithm designers and programmers) can and presumably will be introduced into the algorithms.

An entertaining example of how biases are unconsciously embedded in supposedly objective and automated algorithms is the first international beauty queen contest judged by robots in 2016. Six thousand face applications were submitted from over 100 countries and were judged by five robots that were programed to focus on five aspects of beauty:

Robot judge one was programed to scan and score the wrinkleless of the faces in a given age group; Robot judge two was programed to scan and count the pimples and pigmentation of the faces; Robot judge three scored people by their similarity to beauty models within their racial group; Robot judge four measured the symmetry of the faces; Robot judge five estimated and scored the difference between the chronological and perceived age of the faces.

The robots chose 44 winning faces from the different age groups, but only one black face and few Asian faces were chosen. It was clear that racial bias was somehow introduced. Alex Zhavoronkov, chief science officer of Beauty.AI, the company that developed the beauty algorithm, explained that "The main problem was that the data the project used to establish standards of attractiveness did not include enough minorities" [cited in Levin, 2016, para. 7]. In other words, the robot judges concluded that light skin is a sign of beauty based on the input data used to develop the algorithm.

Many democratic social systems have laws to ensure freedom of access to all governmental activities, but similarly to the supposedly objective algorithm used to judge beauty, these algorithms are hidden from the public eye and are the property of private companies such as Facebook and Google. Today's algorithms are so complex that they can be described as "black boxes" to outsiders, including journalists. A New York University group of scientists established a research institute "AI NOW" dedicated to examining the social implications of AI. In their 2017 report they presented a list of recommendations that aim to protect the social systems from the dangers of AI algorithms. The first recommendation: "Core public agencies such as those responsible for criminal justice, health care, welfare and education ... should no longer use 'Black Box' AI and algorithmic systems" [Campolo *et al.*, 2017]. In the AI Now report the NYU group calls for extensive research into the bias of algorithms, the creation of rigid standards for the use of AI in government decision making, multidisciplinary research and the development of a code of ethics.

This situation has prompted major international concerns regarding the current lack of transparency of how AI algorithms arrive at decisions they make. According to European Parliament member Marietje Schaake, artificial intelligence and machine learning operating away from public view are increasingly being questioned [Burgess, 2016]. Shaake called for more than oversight and transparency "when algorithms affect human rights, public values or public decision-making", and hopes for a situation in which the rule of law and universal human rights are "baked into the systems of large technology companies" [cited in Burgess, para. 8]. Angela Merkel has echoed her sentiments and called for less secrecy.

"Starting in the summer of 2018 the EU may require that companies be able to give users an explanation for decisions that automated systems reach" [Knight, 2017b, para. 6]. Yet, such analysis may prove impossible for deep learning algorithms that program themselves in the very course of the decision-making process. "It is the interplay of a huge amount of calculations inside a deep neural network that is crucial to higher level pattern recognition and complex decision making, but those calculations are a quagmire of mathematical functions and variables" (para. 18). Tommi Jaakkola, a professor at MIT who works on applications of machine learning, explains the lack of transparency: "If you had a very small neural network, you might be able to understand it ... But once it becomes very large, and it has thousands of units per layer and maybe hundreds of layers, then it becomes quite un-understandable" (para. 18).

It is therefore very important for human journalists to make the study of algorithms, systems dynamics, and related issues an important part of their training and areas of coverage. The Columbia School of Journalism made an important step in this direction by establishing a joint degree between journalism and computer science. This program "aims to provide students with a thorough understanding of how particular fields of computer science relate to journalism practice. "Our goal is to train a new generation of computationally literate journalists (or journalistically literate computer scientists) who will redefine journalism as we know it" [https://journalism.columbia.edu/journalism-computer-science#Over view].

8. The Ethics and Governance of AI Fund

In recognition of the dangers that AI decision-making algorithms' lack of explainability poses to government decision-making transparency, MIT Media Lab and Harvard's Berkman Klein Center founded the Ethics and Governance Fund to study and research a cross-section of AI ethics and governance projects and initiatives on a global basis [Hern, 2017]. The fund supports interdisciplinary research involving the collective insights of social scientists, ethicists, philosophers, faith leaders, economists, lawyers, and policymakers, on the potential harm to society resulting from AI's largely invisible decision-making processes.

LinkedIn founder Reid Hoffman and eBay's founder Pierre Omidyar recently contributed USD 20 million to the new fund, and the Knight Foundation, which puts significant effort into preserving and improving journalism, has also contributed USD 5 million to support research aimed at ensuring the safety of artificial intelligence. Alberto Ibarguen, president of Knight Foundation, said "Since even algorithms have parents and those parents have values that they instill in their algorithmic progeny, we want to influence the outcome by ensuring ethical behavior and governance that includes the interests of the diverse communities that will be affected" (Hern, 2017, para. 6).

The analysis of decision-making processes in social systems is an important function of journalists in a democratic society, not only for understanding the rationale behind the decisions being made, but also for making the decision makers accountable for their decisions. Human journalists must first understand the issues, and then ask the important questions, such as: Who is to be held accountable for wrong decisions made automatically by the AI algorithms?

In summary, human journalists who wish to cover social and political systems in the age of AI must have a basic understanding of how systems operate, and for this end, the cybernetic concept provides a useful framework for analysis. The automatic processes that are required, according to cybernetics, for the survival of organizations and systems in changing environments and social objectives are governed by algorithms, which are themselves subject to human biases, and generally lack reference to unquantifiable information, potentially leading to serious malfunctions and endangering organizations' survival.

Already in 1948, in his now classic volume *Cybernetics*, Weiner cautioned that in any social system, the yearning for power by the owners of the media can prevent the system from achieving its goals. If a cybernetic social system is to achieve its goals, journalists must be free of hidden agendas of power and greed. He stated, "One of the lessons of the present book is that any organism is held together ... by the possession of means for the acquisition and transmission of information ... [yet this] system which more than others should contribute to social homeostasis is thrown directly into the hands of those concerned in the game of power and money, which we have already seen to be one of the chief anti-homeostatic elements in the community" [Wiener, 1949, pp. 187–188].

References

Angwin, J. *et al.* (2016). Machine Bias. ProPublica. Retrieved from: https://www.propublica.org/article/machine-bias-risk-assessments-in-criminal-sentencing

Arab-Ogly, E. A. (1958). Applications of cybernetics in social sciences. *Problem Filosofi*, 5, 138–151.

Burgess, M. (2016). Holding AI to account: will algorithms ever be free from bias if they're created by humans? *Wired*. Retrieved from http://www.wired.co.uk/article/creating-transparent-ai-algorithms-machine-learning

Campolo, A. *et al.* (2017). AI NOW 2017 Report. Retrieved from https://ainowinstitute.org/press-release https://ainowinstitute.org/AI_Now_2017_Report.pdf

Ford, J. F. (1966). Soviet cybernetics and international development. In C. R. Dechert (Ed.), *The Social Impact of Cybernetics* (pp. 161–192). Notre Dame, IN: University of Notre Dame.

Hern, A. (2017). Tech billionaires donate $20m to fund set up to protect society from AI. *The Guardian*. Retrieved from https://www.theguardian.com/technology/2017/jan/11/linkedin-ebay-founders-reid-hoffman-pierre-omidyar-donate-research-ai-safety

Knight, W. (2017a). Put humans at the center of AI. *MIT Technology Review*. Retrieved from https://www.technologyreview.com/s/609060/put-humans-at-the-center-of-ai/

Knight, W. (2017b). The dark secret at the heart of AI. *MIT Technology Review*. Retrieved from https://www.technologyreview.com/s/604087/the-dark-secret-at-the-heart-of-ai/

Krikke, J. (2017). Get ready for Chinese AI with a Confucian bias. *Asia Times*. Retrieved from http://www.atimes.com/get-ready-chinese-ai-confucian-bias/

Kuhn, A. (1974). *The Logic of Social Systems*. San Francisco: Jossey-Bass.

Lemelshtrich Latar, N. (1990). The expression of opinions through the new electronic mass media: An Experimental and Cybernetic View. In N. Moray, W. R. Ferrell, and W. B. Rouse (Eds.), *Robotics, Control and Society* (pp. 187–202). London: Taylor & Francis.

Levin, S. (2016). A beauty contest was judged by AI and the robots didn't like dark skin. *The Guardian*. Retrieved from https://www.theguardian.com/technology/2016/sep/08/artificial-intelligence-beauty-contest-doesnt-like-black-people

Solove, J. D. (2004). *The Digital Person: Technology and Privacy in the Information Age*. New York: New York University Press.

Weber, M. (1922/1978). *Economy and Society: An Outline of Interpretive Sociology*. Berkeley: University of California Press.

Wiener, N. (1949). *Cybernetics*. Cambridge, MA: MIT Press.

Chapter 11

Conclusions

Many leading scientists claim that computers will eventually be able to do everything the human brain is capable of doing — only better. Major research institutions, public and private (IBM, Google, Intel, Microsoft, and leading academic institutions), are attempting to design artificial brains that fully emulate the human brain, notwithstanding the beliefs of many people, including Bill Gates, Elon Musk, and Stephen Hawking, that AI is more dangerous to the human race than the atom bomb. One of the more practical and immediate concerns of artificial intelligence is the loss of human jobs to robots and automation. For journalists, this concern is compounded by the rapid penetration of Artificial Intelligence into all media platforms.

In this book I focus on the following question: Will human journalists be replaced by robot journalists and automation, as some have predicted? I believe that free human journalism is a primary condition for long-term human and social survival. After all, robots will not protect human freedom of expression, conduct investigative journalism to identify corruption and social injustice, investigate the dangers that AI and Internet giants pose to political institutions and consumer privacy, or detect and bring to public awareness unforeseen changes in environmental conditions that could endanger human survival.

Automation is penetrating decision-making processes in countless public and private organizations that seek greater efficiencies as they deal with ever-increasing volumes of data (Chapter 10). Even newsrooms are becoming fully automated (Chapter 5). Such automatic decision-making systems will resist social actions that are inconsistent with the pre-determined objectives of these organizations, leading to social instability. Moreover, such decision-making processes are increasingly opaque: The most advanced algorithms employ deep learning methods that make it impossible to trace why and how important decisions were made by the automated systems, let alone detect the biases and ethics of the programmers who wrote the algorithms.

Human journalists must play the crucial societal role of guardians that protect society and humanity from the dangers posed by AI and automation. But can human journalists survive in the competition against their robot competitors? I have chosen to address this important question by exploring whether there are limits to AI, and if there are, whether such limits create new opportunities and new horizons for human journalists and journalism.

1. Are There Limits to AI?

Two schools of thoughts on this important question were identified: The first group is represented by the founding fathers of AI such as John McCarthy, Herbert Simon, and Marvin Minsky (later joined by Ray Kurzweil and Nobel Laureate Daniel Kahneman), who predicted that there are no limits to AI. The second group includes leading scientists such as John Searle and Margaret Boden, who claim that AI algorithms cannot develop consciousness, sub-conscious, or emotions because the current structure of computer hardware comprises simple electronic logic circuits. Neither can computers develop the kind of irrational behavior that may be essential to high levels of creativity, as claimed by Boden and Andreasen (Chapter 2). These limitations give human journalists a clear advantage in developing and applying the high level of creativity that Boden termed "transformational creativity", which involves a transformation of search spaces into new unexpected trajectories. Douglas Eck of the Magenta AI project at Google seems to support Boden's hierarchy of combinational, exploratory, and transformational creativity: In an interview in September 2017, Eck stated, "I think it is unlikely to me that a machine learning algorithm is going to come along and generate some transformative new way of doing art. I think a person working with this technology might be able to do that ... and I think we are so, so, so far from this AI having a sense of what the world is really like" [cited in Metz, 2017, para. 16]. Somers, an author and programmer, agrees with Eck and describes deep learning, currently the most advanced AI tool available, as a "one-trick pony" that mimics the human brain in a shallow way. He claims that the most recent developments in AI are more engineering than science [Somers, 2017].

Three levels of AI are identified in the literature: Narrow AI, General AI, and Super AI. Narrow AI — the current state-of-the-art — refers to algorithms that can perform a single task and are incapable of integrating AI algorithms from other fields of activity. General AI will be able to process information across conceptual fields and thus resemble human intelligence, while Super AI is the name given to future AI algorithms that are expected to surpass the human brain's creativity in all fields of activity, heralding the Kurzweil's Age of Singularity (Chapter 2).

The current level of AI achieved by the past 70 years of research is limited to the Narrow AI. As Fei Fei Li, director of Stanford University's AI Lab and chief scientist of Google Cloud, describes the current state of the art: "If you look at where we are in AI, I would say it's the great triumph of pattern recognition. It is very task-focused, it lacks contextual awareness, and it lacks the kind of flexible learning that humans have" [cited in Knight, 2017, para. 3]. Poggio, the neuroscientist of the MIT Brain Lab, agrees that we are far away from the General AI stage: that "No one knows to make a broader general intelligence like what human have and you cannot do it by gluing together existing programs that play games or categorise images ... I personally think that the problem of intelligence is the greatest problem in science" [Regalado, 2017].

The fact that General AI remains currently beyond our grasp, however, highlights the important competitive edge that human brains have over artificial brains (Chapter 2). Human journalists alone can go beyond detecting rational patterns in the data, by placing facts and stories into meaningful contexts.

Another important opportunity for human journalists was also identified in the evolving nature of journalists' storytelling platforms and techniques and rapidly changing media behaviors across age groups (Chapter 6). Most current robot journalist companies are concentrating on the automatic production of text narratives, yet in their respective chapters, Einav and Lipson, Galili, and Friedman and Kotzen demonstrate that the new journalistic story has increasingly become a complicated fusion of new technologies including VR, AR, 360° videos, and new applications such as Snapchat and Vine. The new stories contain fewer texts, more video, and greater consumer interactivity and involvement. The ability to integrate new visual technologies and applications in sophisticated ways while at the same time constantly monitoring the new technologies and applications being invented is beyond the current capabilities of robots.

2. Guidelines for Human Journalists in the Age of Robot Journalism

AI offers a host of tools to human journalists to dramatically improve the depth, techniques, and modes of delivery of their stories. Such tools can also ascertain that their stories reach their intended audience in the most appealing format.

We are living in the age of Big Data where either our cell phones or sensors embedded in objects that surround us constantly record what we do: The endless data about us is then stored in unlimited data silos. As a result, social research will be less dependent on what people say in surveys, but rather on what people actually do, which implies no less than a major transformation in social science research.

AI algorithms are being used to constantly "crawl" through data silos to discover new social trends and phenomena as they emerge. Unlike robot journalists that have the capability to detect innumerable patterns in these data, human journalists can ask important and relevant questions that refer to non-quantifiable human experience, including emotions, values, and context-related information (Chapter 2) and make effective use of the powerful new tools that AI is making available. The chapter on the journalistic coverage of wars illustrates how human journalists can make effective use of sophisticated and innovative AI applications (Chapter 8).

Human journalists who wish to cover social and political systems in the age of AI must have a basic understanding of how systems operate in the AI era. The cybernetic concept provides a useful framework for analysis (Chapter 10). We have seen that large organizations in the age of Big Data must introduce automation for their survival. These automatic processes are governed by algorithms, which are themselves subject to human biases and errors with serious repercussions — and yet it is not possible to trace how decisions were made. Moreover, not all phenomena important to the function of human society can be quantified and therefore will be ignored by such automatic processes. Journalists must be aware of these serious shortcomings of automation.

AI algorithms enabled the creation of Internet giants such as Amazon, Facebook, Microsoft, and Google, which possess unlimited data silos on every citizen in society and have the potential to become more powerful than governments. The only way to protect democracy from their enormous power is through regulation and transparency. Free human journalism is crucial in this respect: Human journalists must be aware and make their readers aware of these invisible processes and their dangers.

3. The Dangers of AI to Journalists' Freedom of Expression

Media organizations that employ human journalists are able to measure the ROI (Return on Investment) of each journalist they employ and the effects of their stories on audiences, in real time, for example by accessing the number of "likes" or "dislikes" awarded to each individual content unit or even the purchasing behaviors of the readers of the advertised ads placed adjacent to specific journalistic contents. This information can be used by media companies to exert pressure on journalists to tone and tweak their stories to improve ROI figures.

The emergence of digital identities suggests that not only publishers but also journalists themselves will be able to simulate and measure how their stories and storytelling methods impact audiences and other stakeholders, even as the stories are being created. Digital identities of media consumers and the interests of contextual advertisers will introduce tempting opportunities and ethical challenges for human journalists who wish to increase their ROI and story appeal.

In their search for efficiency and to prevent collapse caused by information overload in the age of Big Data, all social organizations have wholeheartedly embraced AI algorithms and automation, unintentionally creating potentially dangerous effects that remain invisible due to the complex nature of these algorithms and the growing strength of digital conglomerates. It is the unique task of human journalism to make the public aware of these dangers. However, in order to fill this role and survive their competition with robot counterparts, human journalists must understand the new media ecosystem and the limits of AI. They must use the emerging new AI tools and applications as tools of their own empowerment, and sharpen their skills of producing highly creative media contents that appeal to consumers' ever-changing media consumption preferences. It is the objective of this book to aid human journalists in making this transition to the age of AI.

References

Knight, W. (2017). The dark secret at the heart of AI. *MIT Technology Review*. Retrieved from https://www.technologyreview.com/s/604087/the-dark-secret-at-the-heart-of-ai/

Metz, C. (2017). How A.I. is creating building blocks to reshape music and art. *The New York Times*. Retrieved from https://www.nytimes.com/2017/08/14/arts/design/google-how-ai-creates-new-music-and-new-artists-project-magenta.html?_r=0

Regalado, A. (2017). Despite all our fancy AI, solving intelligence remains the greatest problem in science. *Technology Review*, Nov 7 2017. Retrieved from https://www.technologyreview.com/s/609330/despite-all-of-our-fancy-ai-solving-intelligence-remains-the-greatest-problem-inscience/

Somers, J. (2017). Is AI riding a one-trick pony? *MIT Technology Review*. Retrieved from https://www.technologyreview.com/s/608911/is-ai-riding-a-one-trick-pony/

Index

www.ingramcontent.com/pod-product-compliance
Lightning Source LLC
Chambersburg PA
CBHW081519190326
41458CB00015B/5403